Glutton

The Multi-Course Life
of a Very Greedy Boy

ED GAMBLE

bantam

TRANSWORLD PUBLISHERS

Penguin Random House, One Embassy Gardens,
8 Viaduct Gardens, London SW11 7BW
www.penguin.co.uk

Transworld is part of the Penguin Random House group of companies
whose addresses can be found at global.penguinrandomhouse.com

First published in Great Britain in 2023 by Bantam
an imprint of Transworld Publishers

A CIP catalogue record for this book is available from the British Library.

ISBNS
9781787636316 (hb)
9780857505521 (tpb)

Typeset in 12.5/17.5pt Sabon MT Pro by Jouve (UK), Milton Keynes
Printed and bound in Great Britain by Clays Ltd, Elcograf S.p.A.

The authorized representative in the EEA is Penguin Random House Ireland,
Morrison Chambers, 32 Nassau Street, Dublin D02 YH68.

Penguin Random House is committed to a sustainable future
for our business, our readers and our planet. This book is made
from Forest Stewardship Council® certified paper.

For Charlie,
who wouldn't let me dedicate
the book to the cat

CONTENTS

I

STARTERS

My obsession with food is lifelong. The stereotypical image of a child is one of the fussy eater, rejecting most things that are put in front of them, catapulting bowls across the kitchen, and puckering their faces at the merest hint of a new taste. This was not me. The bowls stayed on the high chair and my face wore a fixed grin, gratefully receiving spoonful after spoonful of whatever new and exciting purée I could lay my chubby little paws on. Most families have a hilarious photo of their child covered in food, the sort of photo that is brought out at gatherings, or as a way to embarrass someone in front of a new partner. There exists no such photo of me. Not a drop was wasted from plate to mouth, and the front of my baby-grows remained absolutely spotless. (Although I am reliably informed that the back of my baby-grows were a different story.)

My mum tells me on a regular basis that my mouth was 'bigger than all the other babies' and easily devoured anything that was wafted in front of it. Come to think about it, I have made the assumption that she was saying my mouth was bigger than all the other babies' mouths. She could've been suggesting that my mouth alone was bigger than other entire babies. While this does sound believable given the little guzzler I apparently was, I'm sure if it were the case I would've made the news. There would be a newspaper clipping proudly displayed in a family scrapbook. 'Baby's Mouth the Size of Other Babies!' 'There's no need to open wide for the choo-choo train with this little fella, he could swallow a train with ease!' Kriss Akabusi would have squawked on *Record Breakers*. 'I can tell that baby's mine from the cavernous mouth' the caption on *Jeremy Kyle* would've read. Anyway, let's not get bogged down in what ifs – I was a normal-sized baby with a larger than average mouth.

I was as close to being a foodie as one can be as an infant. If I'd had access to Instagram as a baby, I would have been posting pictures of breast milk to my stories. 'OMG, such a great meal at Mum's Boob – you guys have GOT to check this place out.' There was no food I didn't like. My friends would baulk at tomatoes, wince at fish and turn their noses up at peas. I welcomed it all, eager to stuff my face with all my parents had to offer.

Celery was the only thing I refused to eat, and I'm fairly sure that's because I instinctively knew that it was calorie negative. I am only a recent convert to celery, and only then after I worked out that its shape makes it a perfect vehicle for peanut butter. It's essentially an edible spoon, and hence a cheap way of turning even the laziest home cook into a wild and experimental Heston Blumenthal figure. Prior to the celery discovery, I was simply digging peanut butter out of the jar with my finger. After one too many times hungrily trying to bite through my own flesh, though, I turned to my former enemy. But celery on its own still disgusts me. It tastes simultaneously of nothing and every-thing, and as such should not be trusted. 'It's mainly water!' I hear you cry. Well, firstly, stop crying. And secondly, if I gave you a glass of water that tasted like celery, you would quite rightly hurl it back into my stupid face. 'It burns more calories eating it than it has in it!' Well, then it's a waste of time. I'd rather just mime eating something, burn my three calories and never have bothered my mouth with that stringy monstrosity.

If my parents had a suspicion that they had spawned an eater, this was all but confirmed when the time came to take me to restaurants. Given the choice of what to eat, it was painfully obvious that I wasn't going to toe the line: the kids' menu was swiftly rejected out of hand. I feel safe in saying that I never once chose anything from one of those patronizing lists of misery. Even as young as four I had drawn a line in the sand. My mum remembers dis-tinctly taking me for a pub lunch with my grandparents (Nanny and Grandad to me, Steve and Doreen Gamble to you), and Nanny spotting that the pub had a kids' menu. As any right-minded grandma would do, she let me know. I responded, 'I don't DO kids' menus.' As a frugal woman who still essentially practised wartime rationing in her house, I suspect this attitude was quite a shock to Doreen.

She took it in her stride, though, no doubt silently worried that my mother had produced a monster, and got used to it. Just a couple of years later, while at their house for lunch, I proclaimed that her mashed potatoes were pleasant, but I had heard that Gary Rhodes used double cream in his. The word 'precocious' springs to mind, shortly before the words 'little' and 'shit'.

I still don't stand by the concept of kids' menus. Rather than them being needed because children are fussy, I believe that it's the very existence of the kids' menu that creates fussy eaters. I'll put my flag in the ground here and now: they should be abolished worldwide. I believe that given half the chance and the right introduction, most kids would happily just eat what adults eat, rather than the sad offerings that are laid in front of them at most restaurants. I hated being talked down to as a child – why couldn't I have what all the adults had? Fish fingers, onion rings, chicken nuggets, chips, potato waffles – all represented to me an injustice at the dinner table. The adults would order whatever they liked, free to roam the expanse of the main menu, while anyone below the age of ten was fenced into a pen of salty sadness. In my mind, adult food was all excitement and colour, while the kids' choices were a homogeneous and unnatural golden hue.

As you can see, even I have been brainwashed into using the term 'golden' to describe these fried morsels, when this couldn't be further from the truth. Treasure is golden, Labradors are golden. Fish fingers? Fake-tan orange. If treasure or Labradors were the same 'golden' that fried food purports to be, you would leave it buried and have it put down respectively. The kids' menu is not a worthwhile culinary endeavour. If it were, restaurants wouldn't have to provide activities with it to distract the child. 'Don't worry that all the food is the same shade, we'll be providing the colour with this free pack of Crayola!' Nothing made me less excited for a meal as a child than the pressure to complete a word search with a crayon that was simultaneously too thick and too fragile for the task.

I'm not saying that we should be giving six-year-olds oysters (although I'm sure I would've jumped at the chance to try one), I just think we should give them a little more credit. I'm happy to ease the transition by abolishing menu items one by one. First against the wall? The potato smiley. Never has a happy face been less appropriate. A sad, tasteless lump fixed in a rigor mortis grin, which I always think of less as a potato smiley and more as a potato grimace, the potato's face awkwardly contorted in shock at what has become of it. The smiley face, of course, was later embraced by rave culture and acid house, and although not a drugsman myself, I am led to believe there was a lot more reason for the smile in this instance.

Of course, I could be wrong. Maybe most children do enjoy the food on kids' menus, and I was just a weird fat little snob baby. That will be a running theme in this book – the fact that I could be wrong, that is. We considered *This Could Be Wrong* as a title, before speaking to lawyers who told us that legally we couldn't, as that title suggests I might be right some of the time. History has proved that I am wrong almost 90 per cent of the time. This is probably one of those instances. Even as I was writing this diatribe about kids' menus, I floated my hateful theories to my wife. The response went something like this: 'Loads of people like fish fingers, Ed. Just because you were born a puffed-up Little Lord Fauntleroy, it doesn't mean everyone else was.'

And yes, there is some evidence to suggest that I was not a 'normal' child when it came to food. (Or generally, but that's a different book.) Exhibit A: At the wedding of one of my dad's friends, a seven-year-old me sensed injustice when I was informed that there was a separate buffet for the children. Ever the noble agitator, I led a rebellion on behalf of the other kids. They were weak and feeble, crushed by the yoke of adult tyranny. They sat there munching on their nuggets, doing their best job of pretending to enjoy them. Some of them, to be fair, were putting on a pretty convincing performance. They were going the whole nine yards – making approving noises, gleefully dipping away into pots of ketchup, some of them even going back for more! These poor, broken fools. Their commitment to the role was such that they even looked at me strangely when I bravely spoke up to the caterers about the culinary dis-crimination at work. Sure, there was some resistance from our aproned overlords, but no true change is won without a battle. After a short fracas where phrases like 'allocated meals', 'why won't you just eat nuggets?' and 'I'll have to get the bride' were thrown about, and a minor interven-tion from my father, I'm happy to say that the day was mine. Yes, I lost many things that day: potential friends, future work for my father and my temper. But what I gained cannot be overstated. A lovely piece of poached salmon.

I recently recounted this tale to my mum, framing it as the first time I tasted poached salmon (we have good chats). She corrected me and told me that that momentous occasion actually occurred when I was eight months old, at a party hosted by her friend from antenatal class. Apparently my 'eyes lit up', I tucked in, and everyone else was 'very impressed'. I wager that far from being impressed, the other mothers were instead quite perturbed that she had birthed such an odd little gobbler. Meeting me as an infant must've felt like being in *The Omen*, but rather than my parents producing the spawn of Satan, they had somehow created a pint-sized Jay Rayner. (And yes, you are correct. This is the only book you will ever read where the opening pages about the author's childhood feature two stories based around poached salmon.)

I'm happy to say that now, I embrace all of the golden foods. I seem to have evolved my tastes in an odd way. As a child I was eager to show that I could play with the adults, desperate to break the onion-ring handcuffs of culinary oppression. Later in life, though, I welcomed back the comforting tastes of fish fingers, oven chips and chicken nuggets. Not the potato smileys though. They can still fuck off.

As a child I was always very welcome at my friends' houses. Not by my friends, necessarily, but by their mums. The majority of them were raising your classic bog-standard nuggets children. Day after day of cooking the same things for fussy little snotballs who would only eat about four different meals and rejected vegetables out of hand, turning their noses up at anything that was outside their pathetic ten-year-old worldview. So as you can imagine, a visit from me was like a breath of fresh air. I would appreciatively gobble down anything that was put in front of me, pausing only for breaths (fewer than I should probably have taken) and to wheeze regular thank yous through my fat red mouth. I spent much less time with my friends on these playdates than I did in the kitchen with their mums. If the food kept coming, I was going nowhere.

I have never been a one-helping sort of person and that started at a very early age. To this day, I do not understand the one-helping people. If you like something and there is more of it, then why on earth would you not have a second (even a third) helping? You're telling me there are people who have one helping, enjoy it and then sleep soundly without the constant feeling that they've missed out? There is nothing more tragic than the realization that you've eaten something that you might never get to have again, so you need to pack as much of it as you can into your body while you have the chance. On one occasion I was at a friend's house after school and his mum made me round after round of toast slathered in peanut butter. Every time she offered, I said yes. And every time I ate another slice, she would offer me more. For me, this was heaven. For her, it was probably some bizarre scientific experiment to see how many loaves she could get through before this alien child exploded. But I was never one to back down. We were engaged in a toast

stand-off from which she was never going to emerge victorious. I hesitate to call it a game of 'peanut butter chicken',
because peanut butter chicken is basically chicken satay . . .
and that's got me thinking about ordering a Thai meal
tonight. Food threatens to be the downfall of this entire
book. Writing about food makes me think about food and
that will stop me writing this book about food. The whole
thing is a vicious circle. You know what else is a circle?
Calamari. I'm going to get calamari tonight. Oh God.
Anyway, eventually she ran out of bread. I won. She gently
suggested I go and join her son and play some N64 as he
had been alone out there for upwards of an hour.

Being a parent and having your kid's friends over must be
a huge weight off your shoulders for an afternoon. You
have none of the long-term responsibility you have to your
own offspring when it comes to activities like gaming and,
especially, food consumption. They want to eat twelve
slices of toast? Yeah, bollocks to it. Give them an entire bag
of Haribo just before they leave – it's not you who has to
deal with the consequences. In fact, there's a pack of cigs
in the second drawer down and no parental controls on the
internet, you go for it! You're not my kid. In fact, it's pure
advantage for your own child. If your son isn't doing well
at school, invite the cleverest boy in the class over the night
before an exam, load him up on pizza and sugar and watch
him tank the next day due to lack of sleep. Leave the whisky
open on the side for good measure. That way at least your
child is guaranteed to be one place up the school's league
table. But I digress.

This habit is not something that ended after my primary-school years. Even long into being a teenager I would often find myself the willing victim of a feeder parent. I have many memories of being at parent-sanctioned house parties and while chaotic drunkenness and unremitting horniness raged in another room, there I was talking to someone's mother while they prepared me a cheese sandwich.

Being at other people's houses was always a great opportunity to get my way with food away from my mother's gaze. I couldn't get away with it at Steve and Doreen Gamble's house, but I had a much easier ride at the house of my mum's parents, May and Rod Piddock. My grandma was a wonderful cook, nailing all of the classic comfort meals like a pro but also in the way that only a grandma can. No-frills, delicious and filling staples like roast dinners, sausage rolls and something called bacon pudding, which to this day I think I might've dreamt. It was essentially a big Christmas-pudding-sized suet dumpling with chunks of bacon throughout. Hearty and salty with more than enough stodge to go round. The sort of meal you would eat before going out to plough a field. Very rarely when I was at my grandma and grandpa's house, though, did I plough a field after dinner. I mainly just watched *The Velveteen Rabbit* for the thirtieth time, normally with a stomach ache.

I'd say that's always been the problem with my diet: I eat like someone who is halfway through a day of heavy manual labour. The lifestyle of a comedian is relatively sedentary. A lot of time spent on trains, in cars, or sat backstage. The only physical activity our jobs require regularly is up to an hour onstage, and that isn't quite enough to justify the sort of meals that would normally be eaten by a scaffolder or dry-stone-wall builder. I used to suspect that being onstage burnt a lot of calories, so I decided to check my step count for a full show. Seventy-four. In an hour. It's better than nothing, I suppose, but given that I'd driven to the gig and it only increased my day's total to 126 it didn't feel enough to justify the gargantuan beef stew I ate when I got home.

Everyone's grandma's food is a special thing. May Piddock was an extremely caring and loving woman, energetic and passionate to her last day. She was a teacher who was beloved and feared by her students in equal measure. All of the love and attention she put into her job and family was evident in her food, and that's something that even the best professional chefs struggle to capture. If you presented the sort of thing grandmas cook to a Michelin-starred chef as a potential menu item you would be laughed out of the kitchen. Professional kitchens are all about precision, skill and exacting standards. I think they're missing a trick. If there was a restaurant run exclusively by grandmas it would be booked out night after night, full of diners desperate for a taste of that warmth and nostalgia you simply can't get from a steak tartare or a scallop foam. Yes, the service might leave a little to be desired, and it would have to shut at 5 p.m., but it would be a hit!

May Piddock's ham would definitely be the star of the menu. Every year for Christmas she would prepare the most amazing gammon joint. You know by now that as a child I was essentially a tiny Tudor king, so a gammon joint was my idea of heaven. Salty and unctuous meat surrounded by a layer of juicy fat and then enrobed in a sweet and sticky glaze. It was the highlight of my year. We would have it for breakfast on Christmas morning and the day would frankly be impossible to top after that. As I grew older I got into the dangerous habit of going out drinking on Christmas Eve. Inevitably this would lead to furious late-night snacking, which when the fridge is full of carefully prepared food specifically for the next day's festivities is a recipe for disaster. The year I ate all the fat off the ham was not a happy one. The fat is my mum's favourite bit as well, so she had gone to bed hours earlier, happy and contented in the promise of a slice of that sweet treat alongside a fried egg the following morning. Little did she know her drunken oaf of a son would stumble in at midnight, ravenous after a night on the Guinness, and proceed to remove that joyful lardaceous layer with all the care and precision of a backstreet plastic surgeon. I had it on toast. Sorry, Mum, but I'd do it again.

I was thirty-three when my grandma died. Comparatively, this is quite late on in life to lose a grandparent. I was lucky enough to have a full set of them until my thirties, which feels unusual. I remember that all of my school friends lost at least one before we graduated. It's not a competition (and it would be a dark one if it was), but I won. Unfortunately, all that extra time that I got to spend with my grandparents has been paid back in recent years and they've all died. Devastating, of course, but also extremely efficient of them. After my grandma died, I can't pretend that the lack of ham didn't cross my mind. It certainly wasn't the first thought I had when I got the news, but it was probably in the first ten thoughts. I've never said that out loud, let alone written it down, and I'll be the first to admit that it doesn't paint me in the best light. But that's just how good that ham was. The first Christmas after she went was a hard one. I think we all have that person in our life who truly represents Christmas, and that's who she was to me. My grandma *was* Christmas in our family. It was especially hard on my mum and her siblings of course – they had lost their mum. But I had lost my ham.

So that Christmas I decided, as a heartfelt tribute (with a delicious and selfish bonus), I was going to make a ham in her honour. I ordered a joint of gammon months in advance, got all the intel I could on the recipe and set about creating an edible homage to a great woman. It was a disaster. I made the fatal error of snipping the butcher's string off before I put it in the pan, which meant it unfurled in the water like a big pink sea snake and somehow broke into two pieces. I used this to my advantage and tried out a different glaze on each of the slabs. Both awful. One of them gritty with solid sugar and the other burnt within an inch of its life until it was a bitter black mess. All in all, the worst meaty obituary that anyone could conceive of. Not only is it painful enough to have a recipe go so badly awry, I had to deal with the added devastation that I had somehow offended the memory of a dead relative. It all worked out for the best, though, as my mum assured me that Grandma would've found it hilarious, and this was a much better option than discovering I could do a better ham than her. Sometimes things are best just left as a wonderful memory.

My grandpa Rod was less of a natural chef. I think that tends to happen when you are married to someone who is a whizz in the kitchen and doesn't mind doing it – you simply don't need to sharpen that tool yourself. (I say this confidently as the cook in my house.) He was a wonderful man. Gentle, kind, and to date the most relaxed man I've ever met. He used to be a policeman, which I always struggled to imagine. Presumably he was fired after letting multiple criminals go so he could get home in time for his bacon pudding. Some of my warmest and safest memories are of sitting with him in his living room after everyone else had gone to bed. There was never any conversation, just a wholly comfortable and satisfied silence. That silence was eventually broken when he was positive that his wife had gone to sleep. That was his cue to shuffle out to the kitchen and pour himself a whisky. As a kid, I remember thinking that cheeky night-time whisky was the most alluring-looking drink I had ever seen. Just a small amount of brown liquid in a glass seemed to bring him such quiet happiness. On the day of his funeral, some of the family went back to his house to collect a few things. My grandma had also recently passed so it was a day of goodbyes. A goodbye to him, a goodbye to them as amazing grandparents, and there was a realization that this was also a goodbye to a house that was filled with so many memories. I found a bottle of his whisky in the kitchen and, being a sentimental old sod, poured myself a glass to raise to his memory and finally experience what I had seen him enjoy so many times as a boy. It was absolutely disgusting. He really had very cheap taste. I should've learnt from the ham – sometimes memories are enough. You don't need to make grand statements to honour people's passing. Life isn't a film.

My grandpa's bad taste extended to his cooking skills. Aside from late-night sandwiches and whisky, there is only one attempt in the kitchen on record. It's a story that gets dragged out every Christmas in our family. When he was alive it was used to gently ridicule him, but now he has passed the same story is used as a warm and fond memory. Amazing how these things can change. Now bear in mind that this meal he cooked was long before I was born. Yes, he cooked one meal fifty years ago that was so spectacularly bad our family still remembers it. That's almost more of a skill than cooking something successfully. The meal in question was cod fillets cooked in a pan of beer. That's it. That's the meal. For years I've tried to extract as many details about the story from the various family members who experienced it, convinced there must be more to it than that. Some vegetables perhaps? A dash of cream? Salt and pepper, surely? But no. I'm assured it was just cod fillets cooked in a pan of beer. And knowing what sort of beer my grandpa preferred, it would've been Boddingtons. Essentially, a dish of fish in brown foam, which I'm reliably informed had dominant flavours of 'fish' and 'brown'. My favourite part of this story? It was a recipe he had found in a book and it was called 'Tipsy Cod'. The past was wild.

His lack of food knowledge and complete ignorance of what children should be eating made him very easy to bend to my will. My mum, still horrified, recently recounted to me an occasion when she went away on holiday and left me at that house with my grandparents. She returned from that trip and witnessed me sat on the sofa like a four-year-old emperor, ordering Grandpa to fetch me a Coca-Cola. Not too unusual, you might think? Well, it was 8 a.m. and, worst of all, he brought it to me. Lord knows how many mornings that had happened, but knowing myself, I would hazard a guess at every single one, starting immediately after she left. I guess we can just be thankful my grandma was doing the cooking, otherwise Mum would've been welcomed by a pissed toddler who stank of fish and Boddingtons.

This attitude I had to consumption, even at such a young age, would never slow down. Many members of my family used to refer to me affectionately as a 'bottomless pit', presumably in the hope that I would eventually discover the bottom of said pit. How wrong they were. I am no quitter, and my childhood gorging was merely a warm-up for the ensuing years of utter dietary domination.

2

THE BIG GAMBLE

The male Gamble appetite is legendary. Not globally, granted. It's legendary specifically among the female Gambles, who all find it disgusting. Every single man in the Gamble family is the same shape. Blessed with broad shoulders but also cursed with a love of food that is determined to make our waists even broader. During the First World War, we would've been the ones tasked with carrying all the equipment, before being court-martialled for eating all the rations. When we get together, there really is no stopping us. Barbecues are where we do some of our best work. My brother, my dad and I have a splinter WhatsApp group away from the main family group specifically for the discussion and documentation of meat cookery. It's called 'The BBQ Boys', and I love it. Scrolling through it now, there are very few words, just picture after picture of cooked beef, pork and chicken. Very rarely do the photos get a response from anyone. Occasionally I will say 'looks great', but mainly it's a photo followed by a two- to three-week silence until someone else cooks a steak. The BBQ Boys will not sully the group with pandering messages or frothy chat. It is a pure and holy place strictly for the appreciation of meat cookery, and this temple shall not be disturbed with such trivial things as asking after each other's health and happiness or discussing feelings.

The barbecues themselves are 'gross' (a direct quote from my stepmum, Julie, who will normally vacate the premises when my dad announces we are having one). There is something about the introduction of a naked flame that makes the average British man cook far too much. If you were using the oven indoors, you would happily just cook sausages and leave it at that. That is a reasonable dinner. But when we cook over fire, sausages are just the opening salvo. They're barely even considered food – the sausage is more of a flame-temperature tester before we proceed with the bulk of the meal. Do the sausages turn jet black? Well then, the grill isn't ready to be used. Will we eat them anyway? Of course. Stood up at the barbecue, teeth straining to penetrate the tough charcoal-armoured layer until we hit that cool and dangerously pink centre. Then, the real cooking begins. Entire chickens, pork steaks, lamb kebabs, ribeye steaks, burgers, spare ribs – the whole thing starts to look like a *Game of Thrones* banquet (minus incest, plus halloumi).

This attitude has carried over when I do my own barbecues at home. There's something about starting a fire that makes me not want to waste it. I've often put it down to a caveman survival instinct. I have gone to the effort to make this fire, this magical life-giving force. Who knows when we will see this again? So I must use it for all it's worth and cook for the whole tribe. But in truth, it isn't that. It's not a lot of effort to start a fire. I have firelighters. And I'm not a member of a tribe, it's just me and my wife, and she can take or leave most meat. It's simply that I approach food like every male member of my family – I eat like it is my last meal on Earth.

My appetite led me to be branded all sorts of things growing up. 'Human dustbin', 'Gobbletron 5000', 'unstoppable pig person' – you know, the classics. I was also regularly told 'Your eyes are bigger than your stomach.' This is a peculiar phrase that is used to describe someone who gets overexcited and overloads their plate. Their eyes widen at the sheer possibility of everything they could be eating, and they fail to take into account that they couldn't possibly fit it all into their stomach. Not, as I used to assume, that the person in question has ginormous eyes. This doesn't work as a phrase. Once I established what it meant I took it as a challenge to prove that while, yes, my eyes were big, my stomach was more than up to the job. To this day, I have never had leftovers. But when I first heard this phrase as a child, I distinctly remember being petrified. The art of metaphor is slightly beyond us in the early stages of life, so we tend to take language fairly literally. Imagine for a moment someone with eyes bigger than their stomach. Multiple images rush through your mind all at once. The first is of someone with massive eyes. As a kid, I wasn't exactly sure how big stomachs were, but I was fairly positive that they were much bigger than eyes. The idea of some dopey-looking bug-eyed monster lolloping about the place filled me with dread. What if he cried? We'd all surely drown! How big would his glasses have to be? Awful. That person's appetite would be the least of everyone's concerns. 'He's got eyes bigger than his stomach' wouldn't be a careless and derogatory phrase to describe someone's greed but the first thing you should tell the 999 operator. I'd imagine that the conversation would go something like this.

Operator: '999, which service do you require?'

Caller: 'I don't know actually.'

Operator: 'Well, what appears to be the problem?'

Caller: 'It's this man I've just found . . . his eyes are bigger than his stomach.'

Operator: 'Do you mean he has a larger than average appetite? That's not really something you should be calling about.'

Caller: 'No, I mean his eyes are huge. I'm actually a bit worried about his appetite because he can barely lift his head to eat.'

At that point, I'd imagine the 999 operator would hang up. I say 'imagine', but that's exactly what happened to me when I tried it. A huge and irresponsible waste of resources, sure, but invaluable book research.

We also have to consider the idea that the phrase could be describing someone with a stomach so minuscule that it is smaller than the average human eye. This, for me as a child, was an even scarier prospect. Such a person could never be accused of being greedy – every meal they ever had would have to be eye-sized. Breakfast would be a raisin, lunch would be a quail's egg, and dinner a single grape, or a brazil nut if they were feeling fancy. For some people, this probably sounds ideal, being able to nibble on something they fancy until they don't want any more and they can go about their day. For me, food has never been about eating until I am satisfied. I would go so far as to say that I have never experienced a feeling of satisfaction after a meal. I either finish a meal still hungry or, more often than not, uncomfortably full. The times I stop eating still hungry are those rare occasions when I feel it would be polite to do so – when meeting new people, for example. On my first date with Charlie, now my wife, we only had a main course. This is unthinkable now. It's called the main course for a reason: for it to be considered the 'main' one it has to be accompanied by other courses. If it was meant to be the only course, it would be called just that. But on a first date, you want to look like you are a delicate and considered person, not someone who consumes food like Obelix. What I'm saying is – I can eat. I become overwhelmed with the sheer choice and wonder of food and I have to get it all in my mouth immediately. There is a certain amount of panic involved – what if I never come back to this place again? This might be my only opportunity! Well, calm down, Ed, you're in Pizza Express – put down the dough balls.

I'll spend much of this chapter talking about being over-weight. I'm sure many of you will exclaim something like,

'But you aren't fat, Ed, what are you talking about? How dare you discuss an issue that doesn't affect you!' And then probably murmur something about fat appropriation. I know, I know, I'm not overweight now – but I assure you I was. Just imagine the guy on the cover of this book (me) has been put through one of those apps that make you look fat. Quite a complicated way to describe all this, but I stand by it. I can't stress this enough: I was a very fat child. But, guess what? I *loved* being a fat child.

Being fat actually isn't an issue socially when you are little. People LOVE fat babies. There is nothing that delights people more than meeting a baby with chubby cheeks, a round tummy and those weird fat arms that look like three sausages smooshed together. They gently pinch your folds and grab your cheeks as if you are some sort of living good-luck charm. A baby with an appetite is seen as healthy and happy. People say things like, 'Oh, he likes his food, doesn't he!' or 'That little belly is so adorable' and, more disturbingly, as I heard once, 'She looks like a mini Winston Churchill!' This appreciation of plumpness lasts throughout toddlerhood. After all, there is no finer sight than a stout two-year-old waddling about in dungarees before losing their balance and plopping down on to their ample rear.

But at some point, attitudes change. Without warning, your shapely midriff that was once so venerated by family and visitors isn't sweet any more. It is a cause for concern. It is no longer that wonderful 'baby fat', it is just 'fat'. And people really don't like that. I'm not saying I feel like I should've been treated the same as a fat baby when I was a fat fifteen-year-old. The cheek-pinching wouldn't have been ideal and I wouldn't have liked anyone laughing at my dungarees (I did have a pair though). I'm simply saying that some warning would've been nice. It's very confusing and jarring to find out one day that your body shape suddenly attracts criticism. A lot of people find that they naturally grow out of that phase, of course. Fat little babies and toddlers who shed their flesh cocoons and emerge as wonderful butterflies, free to flutter their way through school, university and beyond, living sparkling lives full of small meals and regular sex. Some of us, on the other hand, hold on to our cocoon. I went from cute chubby baby to adorable waddling toddler to fat goth teenager to obese man in his twenties. This was partly genetics, of course, but mainly my own doing. Like all good sportsmen, I took what God gave me and put the hard yards in at training.

It was when I started secondary school that I realized I was fat. This isn't going to be a sob story – I was in the main very happy. Among the privileges that boys have is being able to make body shape part of their personality. I cottoned on quickly that to fit in with any social group I was going to have to make chub part of my brand. Luckily, 'funny fat guy' is a pre-established crew member in all aspects of pop culture. Every Hollywood film from the 1980s and 1990s had a big kid whose job it was to wear a loud shirt and say something funny before inevitably dropping his sandwich and farting. (Not that I would ever, ever drop a sandwich.) There wasn't a lot of dignity involved, but I was willing to do whatever the role demanded. You don't need dignity at school, you just need friends.

Being the funny fat guy came pretty easily. The fat looked after itself really – it was a pleasure to maintain. The funny side of things was pretty simple as well. Being overweight naturally makes you a social underdog, and being a social underdog makes it much easier to be funny. Nobody actually finds the handsome rugby players funny – people laugh at their jokes in order to ingratiate themselves with someone higher in the pecking order. As such, the handsome rugby players go through their school years thinking they're hilarious. Then they get into the real world and . . . well, everyone continues to laugh at their jokes in order to ingratiate themselves with someone higher in the pecking order. Bit annoying, really. There are loads of gorgeous people out there who will die thinking they're hilarious. I, on the other hand, was forced into actually developing a personality and a sense of humour, mainly based around being fat and cheeky. I took some cues from some of the tubby jokers of the silver screen and would often wear loud Hawaiian shirts, or just generally 'amusing' items of clothing. Particularly fetching was an XXXL grey hoodie emblazoned with the words 'Phat Bastard'. This served the dual purpose of making everyone relax and know that, yes, I was aware that I was overweight; alongside finally reclaiming the word 'phat' from 1990s hip-hop groups. It sounds like a cliché, but I used humour as a defence mechanism. After all, there's no way that people could make jokes about my weight if I was making them myself, faster and better. Aside from losing weight, this is the best way to ward off potential bullying in school. And there was absolutely no way I was going to lose weight. I loved food, and plenty of it.

When I first arrived at King's College Wimbledon I was told I had the choice of a packed lunch or canteen dinner. They were forgetting, of course, about the secret third option: 'both'. 'Both' is such a wonderful word when it comes to eating, and the perfect defence against the word that is the scourge of dining: 'or'. Starter or dessert? Both, thanks. Ice cream or custard? Both! Scrambled or fried? OK, maybe that one's a bit weird (though obviously I've tried it: I once had a scrambled and fried egg omelette, which I can heartily recommend if you love feeling ill for forty-eight hours). Why wouldn't you say *both*? Well, in the case of school dinners, I wasn't allowed to because 'the man' didn't like me flicking two fingers up at the system. In this case, 'the man' was whoever was in charge of the school budget, and 'the system' was 'paying' for 'food'.

So began five years of subterfuge and espionage that I have retrospectively named 'Operation Double Dinners'. My mum would dutifully make me a healthy and delicious packed lunch every morning. It was pretty standard fare, put together with thought and love. A regular menu might include a cheese and ham sandwich, a piece of fruit, a bag of crisps and a Club. Thinking about it now, that is a decent packed lunch. A delicate balance of nutrition and fun. At the time I was jealous of the kids whose packed lunches featured things like a whole pack of biscuits or a cold

McDonald's. But looking back on it, the funner the lunch, the more Social Services should probably get involved.

I never really appreciated the lunch my mum made, to the extent that I wouldn't even eat it at lunchtime. No, the whole thing would be demolished at morning break. As soon as the clock hit 11 a.m., the sandwich would be out of the bag and in my face, followed by the crisps and Club. The fruit would occasionally be eaten, but more likely be employed for another use. Bananas were particularly good for bin target practice or wanging at a classmate. I once took my apple to the playground and bowled it at someone during a game of cricket. The flash of red was enough to convince them that it was a ball and they played it beautifully, only to see it explode into hundreds of pieces. You've probably never seen the look on the face of someone who thinks they're hitting a cricket ball but it turns out to be an apple – it's very specific. The key moment is the split second after they've obliterated the apple, when they still think it's a cricket ball. Just for an instant they believe that they are the strongest person in the world, before the crushing truth dawns on them that a cheeky trickster has delivered them a Pink Lady. (I realize this makes it seem like my childhood was a *Just William* book. In truth, I spent most break times sat inside, or smoking.) The long and short of it is, the packed lunch that my dear mother assumed was sustaining me throughout the day was barely making it to 11.05 a.m.

Come lunchtime itself, I would go to the dining hall to get school dinner. This was a school dinner that nobody had paid for and that I absolutely should not have been having. But every day, there I was, piling my plate high with a cornucopia of every shade of beige you can imagine. This was a contrast to my days as a child gourmand, of course. Back then I wouldn't have countenanced the sort of things served in school canteens, but now I was all about quantities and calories. Pre-sliced roast meats smothered in thick brown gloop, roasties that were somehow within the space of a single potato both raw and overcooked, and vegetables that had been boiled for so long that they were no longer identifiable as food. I loved it all.

But my favourite day of the week was Rib Wednesday. 'Rib' is quite a misleading description in this context. School-dinner ribs were a curious item: reconstituted meat formed into long patty-style rectangles, texturally somewhere between the worst burger you've ever had and a washing-up sponge, covered in a sauce so sweet and offensive that you could clean coins in it. The most bizarre thing was the attempt to shape them into a vague rack-of-ribs appearance, as if anyone was going to be fooled that this thing had been removed, as it was, from a pig. I doubt if it had ever been near a pig. The company involved had probably exploited some sort of government loophole. 'I've got it – as long as we spell it "ryb" and get a pig to stare at the packet for over ten seconds, we can legally sell this as meat!'

My fellow students knew about Operation Double Dinners, of course. They would see me annihilating a full lunch at 11 a.m. and then join them for school dinner at 1 p.m. If I had been smarter, I would've concocted some sort of disguise – perhaps a new foreign exchange student.

Ed Gamble having a canteen dinner might be a bit weird, but they would think nothing of Eduardo from Mexico City indulging in jam sponge with custard while politely tipping his sombrero to passing staff members. Honestly, though, there was no need to conceal what I was doing from my peers. Why would I? I was the funny fat guy – this is exactly what I should be doing! Eating copious amounts and cracking wise while I did it. There was something quite powerful about leaning into this social role, and it's definitely played a major part in what I do now. On one occasion I distinctly remember taking twelve Dairylea triangles from the salad bar and trying to eat all of them at once for an assembled crowd who chanted my name and laughed. There's nothing sad about that! I was a hero! Although, reading that sentence back now, maybe there was something sad about it.

By the time I went to university, I was a Fully Formed Funny Fat Guy (FFFFG). If you're expecting this to be the point in the story where I start losing weight, you are going to be sorely disappointed. The absolute worst place to lose weight as an already fat eighteen-year-old is the first year of university. No, I simply went from a FFFFG to a FFFFF – Fully Formed Funny Fat Fresher. When I arrived at Durham University, I heard students casually talking about the 'fresher's fifteen' or 'fresher's flab'. This is something I hadn't come across before. It refers to the fact that during the first year of university, most students put on a significant amount of weight – most of them fifteen pounds or more. Aside from the opportunity to add another F to my title, this wasn't what I wanted to hear. I had more than enough flab, thank you very much. I hadn't yet got round to losing my childhood puppy fat, let alone eighteen years' worth of daily indulgence and Christmas belly worship, and now I had to deal with these mysterious tertiary education gains. The light-hearted way they would talk about it upset me – these skinny rascals all chuckling at the inevitability of putting on weight like it was some sort of rite of passage. Some of us have done it already, I'll have you know! I wasn't at uni to gain weight. I was there to lose my virginity. Well, I did gain weight. The virginity? I'll keep that to myself. (As in, I kept it to myself.) The issue was obvious. I was already big, despite there being some sort of maternal vigilance over my diet at home. Yes, there was Operation Double Dinners, but after school I would go home to my mum, who by and large cooked measured, wholesome meals. I wasn't rebelling against an overly officious healthy-eating parent – my food at home was filling, nutritious and balanced. So as you can imagine, when this was removed from my life when I moved away from home, things came off the rails pretty quickly. And I mean that literally – as soon as I stepped off the train.

Finally, I was free of the shackles of my pesky mother. For too long she had imprisoned me with her insistence upon vegetables, fruit and water. I had been emancipated from her dreadful and oppressive vitamin regime. Now I could roam with abandon from bakery to pizzeria and back to the bakery again, fuelled by a constant stream of cheap lager. Looking back on one of my normal days as a fresher, it sounds like the complete opposite of one of those 'what I do in a day' videos the wellness influencers make.

Hi guys! A lot of you have been asking to see what I do in a regular day, so here it is! Don't forget to like and subscribe – and remember if this video gets 25K likes, I'll release the full film of my colonoscopy! OK, here goes!

8 a.m. – My friend Fiona knocks on my door to tell me she's off to our Philosophy lecture that starts in thirty mins. I grunt something unintelligible until she gives up and leaves me alone. #sleep is important, guys! It's vital to stay well rested to maintain healthy skin and a great attitude!

9.30 a.m. – I am awoken by the desperate urge to #piss. I am living in a room on a corridor with a shared bathroom which is over fifteen steps from my bed. There is a sink two steps away, but only one step if I hop over the bubbly patch of carpet where I spilt shampoo on my first day. It's still early and I've already exercised!

12 p.m. – I roll out of bed (more cardio!) and light a cigarette. I love tobacco! All about that #plantlife!

1 p.m. – Breakfast! I prefer to eat breakfast late, because I intermittently fast. The last thing I ate was a burger at 4 a.m., so my tum is rumbling! Breakfast is the most important meal of the day, it's going to fuel you for the rest of the day! Today I go to Peter's Bakery and have a steak bake, bacon roll and a slice of cheese and tomato pizza.

2 p.m. to 5 p.m. – #coffee, #cigs, #snacks. Got to keep that energy up to avoid my lecturers in case they ask where I've been! Luckily, none of them know who I am anyway.

6 p.m. – It's off to the college bar for #social #interaction. Me and my neighbour Murray are the smoothest guys at our uni, which is why we play it cool and silently drink in the corner, occasionally making snide comments about all the posh rugby players being alcoholics. We drink nine pints of lager. Remember, if you buy draught pints they will most likely be watered down, meaning they are #keto and keep you hydrated!

10 p.m. – We head out clubbing (drinking pints in a different, darker corner). The club in question is Klute. It stinks and is awful. It's important to have a schedule to your day so you can feel a sense of achievement. The next two hours is the time I have allotted to feel sad! But luckily, it's two for one on quadruple vodka and Red Bull, so I take advantage and buy two! I love a deal! I polish off the last one as the lights come up, guaranteeing I won't sleep later. Too much sleep is bad for your skin!

2 a.m. – It's off to the authentic Turkish mezze restaurant Dirty Jane's. I do love to support local business! There are so many Insta-worthy menu items, but tonight I go with cheesy chips

*with doner meat. I have to think about my macros, and I'm yet
to hit my daily target of one kilo of salt, so this should be
perfect!*

*4 a.m. – It's bedtime! A good sleep is dependent on a serene
and #blissful environment, so I like to put my laptop on full
brightness and watch illegally downloaded episodes of Heroes.
Weighted blankets are all the rage for good reason, so I
choose to fall asleep with half a box of cheesy kebab chips on
my chest. Ready to take on whatever the world throws at me
tomorrow!*

This was as close to a normal day as I can remember. A
totally delicious onslaught of calories, alcohol and nico-
tine. The bizarre thing is, I don't ever remember feeling
any ill effects from it. There are any number of explana-
tions for this. The big one is youth. My tender and supple
body could simply soak up all of these toxins, successfully
filter them out and leave me fresh and perky to tackle the
day. Looking at photos of myself from then, however,
would suggest that this was not the case. I look neither
perky nor supple. I wear every single drink and late-night
meal on my pale and puffy face. I somehow simultaneously look like a skull and a meatball, yet I always have a
whacking great smile plastered across my face. It was such
a genuinely wonderful time when I was utterly unencumbered by vanity. I simply ate and drank what I wanted and
got on with it.

Even though my normal days at uni were quite indulgent,

there was one day that even for me stands out. The Day of the Four Pizzas – a huge moment in both my history and that of Durham University. There's a rumour that they may be erecting a blue plaque in the cathedral to commemorate my achievement, but we'll have to wait and see (they've not answered my email asking them to do this).

It started like any other day, at noon (see earlier). Rather than spending my day working on my degree, I had a busy schedule with a comedy-sketch group that I had joined during my first year, the Durham Revue. It was this that took up the majority of my time at university. At the time, I used to justify it by saying that writing comedy was, in its own way, a form of philosophy (the course I should've been focusing on). This argument falls apart when you find out that the sketches used to end mainly with fart sound effects. I will happily now admit that perhaps they didn't contribute hugely to the history of thought. We had a show that evening, and our friend Nick Mohammed was in town to perform with us. Nick is a wonderful man, an excellent comedian, and his favourite restaurant is Bella Italia. I hesitate to reveal this fact, as Nick has since been nominated for an Emmy, and if they catch wind of this they will probably eradicate the nomination from history. The award was eventually won by Brett Goldstein, who has confided in me that he doesn't 'understand' food. It is clearly integral to Emmy success that you don't eat well, and this is the only reason why I will never win one. Being good friends, we decided to accompany Nick to his favourite eatery for lunch, so I selflessly skipped my usual bakery breakfast basket (a BBB for the FFFFF). For those of you who aren't aware of Bella Italia – what have you been eating under your big rock?! It's an authentic Italian *ristorante*, founded by Nonna Bella in Sardinia in 1906. The menu is absolutely packed with age-old recipes handed down through the generations – just like Mamma used to make. I ordered the hoisin-duck pizza.

Hoisin-duck pizza, by anyone's standards, is a step too far. I'm all for a bit of fusion cuisine, but something about combining Italian and Chinese doesn't sit quite right. I'd like to write about this further but every thought I have makes me sound oddly right-wing. I'd like to make it clear that when it comes to human relationships I believe that love is love no matter where you are from, but let's not extend that to putting hoisin sauce on a pizza or chicken tikka in a lasagne (looking at you, Iceland). However, I understand this is all coming across as mighty hypocritical, given that I ordered it. At the time, I was simply eager to pack in as many takeaway foods as possible at all times, and this dish was highly efficient. As far as I was concerned, it could only have been improved with a poppadom base. It's not difficult to describe the taste of the pizza. It was exactly as you'd imagine: dough base, hoisin sauce (instead of tomato, which I begrudgingly admit is quite inventive), mozzarella cheese, roast duck and spring onion. I seem to recall I rolled it up like a pancake and ate the whole thing with my hands as a hilarious joke, but that is potentially my brain punching up my memories.

The terrifying thing is, we're at 3 p.m. by this point and I've only told you about one pizza. You're probably on tenterhooks! How will our hero hit the promised four pizzas by the end of the day? Well, fear not, dear reader! What have you heard so far that makes you doubt that I can squeeze three more pizzas into the rest of my day?

Dinner started off pretty straightforwardly. We all trooped off to a local takeaway to grab a quick bite before the show. These days I cannot eat anything substantial before performing. A pizza before a show would be unthinkable; I would feel weighed down, sluggish and unable to think. Pathetic, really. I hate me now. Fat Ed was a legend, easily putting away a large pepperoni with extra cheese and anchovies and still going out and annihilating a comedy-sketch show in front of upwards of thirty very drunk and easily pleased students.

I know you can count – we're on two pizzas. But when I said that this dinner was straightforward, I lied. After I purchased my dinner, I was invited to spin the wheel. Initially I was baffled. I'd never been in this particular takeaway before, and 'spinning the wheel' was not an offer I'd had in any arena of hospitality before (or since). It was only after the owner offered that I noticed the wheel behind the counter. A big, clearly home-made *Wheel of Fortune*-style prize wheel, with various categories written in each segment. The prizes I remember included £5, a large bottle of soft drink, a tub of ice cream, a month of free pizza (conditions apply) and a free large margherita. Even before

I spun it I knew what was going to happen. My fate was already decided. It was written in the stars. With slow and inevitable determination the wheel clicked slowly round, missing the £5 (would've been handy), the soft drink (my preferred choice), the ice cream (inconvenient) and the month of free pizza (a death sentence) before landing on the free margherita. So I collected my spoils and left that shop with two large pizzas. The pepperoni I dispatched without even thinking about it. I still to this day can eat a pepperoni with extra cheese and anchovies as quickly as anyone else might eat a single grape. The margherita caused a few more issues though.

The overwhelming feeling in you as a reader must now be 'Why didn't you give the pizza away, Ed? Surely there were plenty of students who would've loved to have taken that off your hands?' And to that I say – yep, good point. It's hard to explain, but my fat brain does not allow sharing. I still consider myself to have a fat brain. I cannot share and I cannot order the right amount of food. Because as soon as I am confronted by food, something takes over. I am overcome by some sort of caveman instinct, as if I have been in the wilderness without sustenance for days, so I should now take this opportunity to cram as much of it into my body as possible. The truth is, of course, I've almost certainly eaten ninety minutes earlier. It's completely illogical, yet even to this day it's a hurdle I can't get over. So no, I didn't share the margherita, despite hating a margherita.

A cheese and tomato pizza to me is the ultimate representation of unfulfilled potential. A wonderful canvas, for sure. But how anyone can leave it at that is beyond me. Pizza purists will tell you that is all you need – just tomato, cheese and basil. What an utter waste of creativity – it's like they've never heard of duck! Imagine if the Italians had extended that attitude to their artists? 'Sì, Signore da Vinci, that's a lovely background you've done. You can probably leave it there! I know you wanted to paint a grumpy lady, but that would be crowding what is already a simple and beautiful piece of work!'

I did, however, eat the margherita that night. At the time I didn't realize that I was pushing for a four-pizza day, but I think I had a distant feeling that on my shoulders that night I was carrying history. I ate half immediately after the first (nice) pizza and took the rest to the show, occasionally nibbling at it throughout the evening whenever I came offstage. It's a time other performers might use to change costume or get a prop, but I used it to lob another chunk of now congealing cheesy dough down my neck.

The show was a triumph, as they always were. (I can't tell you how easy it is to perform to an audience of what is essentially drunk friends. It's so easy that it gives you enough confidence to believe that you can seek out a career in the arts after university.) My character of 'man with increasing amount of tomato on his face' went down particularly well, however similar it was to my character of 'man with tomato sauce down his front'. Three pizzas down.

We then all trooped off to the aforementioned nightclub.

It might have stunk and it might have been awful, but Klute was really the only option in Durham at the time. The place was the absolute embodiment of student irony. We're all aware of how much students enjoy doing things ironically. I'd go so far as to say that in my three years of studying, I never did one thing sincerely. When you're eighteen, the funniest thing in the world is acting as if bad stuff is good. It's a culture that has completely sustained the career of Chesney Hawkes. Based only on his song 'The One And Only', he can tour universities playing Freshers' Balls to a rapturous reception. He played our Freshers' Ball and went down a storm when he performed 'The One And Only'. At one point he decided to cover John Lennon's 'Imagine' and somebody threw one of the balls from the ball pit at him. I believe that this was actually quite a nice gig for him, as there were rumours that the week before at Birmingham University the crowd had booed him every time he'd tried to play anything other than 'The One And Only', meaning he ended up playing it eleven times in a row. But when he did, everyone lost their minds. Did anyone mean it? Of course not, they were being ironic. But once ironic adulation hits a certain level, it really doesn't matter whether it's ironic or not. The one thing that isn't ironic is the cheque, and Chesney is laughing (ironic) all the way to the bank (real). Now that I'm in my thirties, I take the controversial stance of 'good stuff is good'. Life is too short to snigger behind your hand at anything. There's such a rich cultural world at our fingertips that it hurts my heart that

I spent so long deliberately seeking out films and music that I knew would be terrible because I thought it would make me some sort of edgy legend. Having said that, I've just popped on a bit of Chesney and it's actually quite good.

Klute, however, was not good. I will never go back there. Imagine the smallest nightclub you have ever been in. Now halve that. Now cover every surface with a sticky sheen so powerful that you have to walk round on tiptoes for fear of spending the rest of the night rooted to the same spot. I would be so crude as to suggest this was some sort of sexual effluvium, but the smell of bleach was so potent that everyone in the room was rendered immediately and completely numb from the waist down. Yet this tiny hellhole was (and so I'm led to believe, still is) the pride of every Durham student. They will all gleefully tell you that it is 'the worst nightclub in Europe'. This seems like an outrageous claim but it is based on some fact. There was indeed an *FHM* poll in the 1990s on Europe's worst nightclub. Klute came second to a dive somewhere in Serbia, which promptly burnt down. That's right – Klute is such an awful place that it couldn't even win an award without the help of fire. Frankly, fire might improve Klute. Aside from Chesney, the playlist was like a vision of Hades from an Ancient Greek myth. It was extremely limited and would be played over and over again until you either left, got onboard or ran headfirst into a wall. I witnessed all three taking place across numerous visits.

Typical Klute playlist (2004–7)

'The One And Only'
Chesney Hawkes

'Chelsea Dagger'
The Fratellis

'Being Sick In A Glass And Then Drinking It'
Rugby Players

'The Fresh Prince Of Bel-Air'
DJ Jazzy Jeff & the Fresh Prince

'Lots Of Laughter, You Think It's Probably At You'
Group of Girls

'In Da Club'
50 Cent

'Shut Up'
Black Eyed Peas

'Shut Up'
Group of Girls (feat. You Asking Why They're
Laughing At You)

'That's Amore'
Dean Martin

At the time I loved it – because a trip to Klute meant a
trip to Dirty Jane's, the brothel-sounding takeaway next
door. Exactly fifteen stumbling steps away, so you could fall
out of Klute, belly full of quaddie voddies (quadruple
vodka shots that were presumably watered down to such
an extent that they were the equivalent of a single), and
headfirst into a polystyrene container of wet chips. The

actual name of the shop was not Dirty Jane's – it was run by a (lovely) lady named Jane, and the food was dirty. I want to make it very clear that at no point does the 'dirty' part of the nickname relate to Jane herself. From what I can remember, she was squeaky clean – remarkably so, given the amount of chip grease that must've been in the air. No, it was the food that was dirty. This was before the trend for 'dirty' food. Hipster fast-food restaurants of the 2010s in particular used to love to proclaim that their food was 'dirty', as if this was a fantastic selling point that we should all be happy with. It was a collective madness we all accepted as completely normal – actual places we were paying money to essentially saying 'Eat this and you'll feel awful, and that's exactly what you deserve, you big slug.' I'm glad the trend waned a little, or I'm confident it would have ended with a high-street burger shack selling us clumps of soil for £15. But not even a SodNugget Muck-Burger™ could out-dirty my final pizza of the day.

It was listed as a 'special' on Jane's board, which I'm fairly sure was short for 'especially disgusting'. It had all the usual suspects pizza-wise, of course – tomato, cheese, olives. But what went on top of that would give an Italian a heart attack (metaphorical) and anyone who ate it a heart attack (actual). Because delicately dumped on to that perfectly pleasant pizza was the biggest pile of doner meat I have ever witnessed, followed by a liberal squirt of both chilli and garlic sauce. Through my drunken haze, this seemed like a perfectly reasonable thing to eat. Jane seemed shocked. She made a face that suggested this was the first time anyone had ordered this particular creation. As if a staff member had come up with the idea as some sort of sick joke – a meal so disgusting and impossible to eat that nobody would ever order it. Well, here I was, ready to punk them straight back.

Watching them build it was when I began to regret my decision. The pile of doner meat being liberally draped across the surface of the pizza was the first time I remember feeling shame connected to food. There would be plenty of that to come in my life, but this first pang was acute and deep. By the time Jane had expertly squirted the chilli and creamy garlic sauces I was just about ready to change my name and emigrate. The only person in history to join the witness protection programme because of extreme and self-inflicted takeaway trauma.

As I watched all four staff members struggle to cram the lid down on this meaty monster, it struck me that I had a few options. The first of which was to realize my mistake and simply run out of the shop. I didn't have to go back; I could just live on as the legend of the man who ordered the forbidden grease bomb, panicked and swiftly exited the shop crying. This, looking back, probably would have been the smartest thing to do. Three years of being known as the weeping kebab-shop coward would almost certainly have been preferable to the inevitable gastric horror of actually consuming what I had asked for. The next option was to take the pizzab (kebizza?), thank the proprietor and calmly leave the shop before throwing it into the river under the cover of night. This was a course of action I genuinely toyed with. I distinctly remember standing on a bridge, holding the box, staring into the dark water and thinking that with one flick of the wrist I could be rid of this cursed object. It's the closest I've ever felt to a murderer looking to dispose of a body. But instead of a murderer, I was a very greedy boy and my corpse was a very greasy pizza.

And when I say greasy, I'm not yet sure you're quite envisaging what I mean. 'Oh, I've had greasy things!' is what you're saying out loud now, like a big weirdo. 'Like when you get a pasty and there are some dark spots on the paper bag!' you continue, despite everyone around you starting to get uncomfortable. Well, let me say now – YOU WEREN'T THERE, MAN! You did not witness the carnage I witnessed. This was my Vietnam. I was the young GI charged with clearing the contents of this box, and the grease spots were the skirmishing soldiers of the Viet Cong (as my GI persona would have known them back then). And they emerged through the undergrowth of the box in a second. The lid immediately changed colour until it became almost transparent. Then secondary grease spots appeared, areas of blackness darker than I had ever witnessed before. It was like staring into the eyes of the purest evil. The grease patches seemed to spell out 'EAT ME' in a horrifying demon font, but that could've been the last quaddie kicking in. It occurs to me that anyone who happened to be walking past and saw a worried-looking student staring over the bridge might've been momentarily concerned that I was undergoing some sort of perilous episode. Upon closer inspection, though, they would've seen I was holding a pizza and changed their mind. Nobody in history has ever committed suicide holding a pizza. (I'm going to request that a lawyer at my publisher check this, just in case there's a tragic backstory to Papa John I'm not aware of.)

In the end I took the final option – going back to my room and eating the pizza. I snuck it back into my halls of residence under my coat like I was a minor celebrity evading the paparazzi with a new squeeze. Once safely inside, I attacked it with the ferocity of a famished vulture that's just spotted a wildebeest carcass, only with more self-hatred. That's a quality you never observe in the animal kingdom. Not once while watching an Attenborough documentary have I ever seen a lion turn to the camera with a look in its eyes that says 'Why am I eating this? It's my fourth antelope of the day. I've got to sort my life out.' But that's definitely the first time I had that thought. There was little else to think after the Day of the Four Pizzas. There was some residual pride, I suppose, but most of that was eradicated by the crushing depression that only extreme amounts of fast food can bring. It would be a few years and a few hundred pizzas until I actually made good on that promise to myself. I'm not going to go into many more of these pizzas – that's a book in itself. Let's just say not one year later I and my partner in crime Murray ordered a fifteen-inch pizza each and his only topping was baked beans. I didn't know it at the time, but the Day of the Four Pizzas was the start of a mental shift that would lead me to start approaching food in a new way.

ALL THE FOOD MASCOTS RATED BY HOW LIKELY THEY ARE TO MURDER YOU

Ronald McDonald

When he first came on the scene, he must've seemed like a cheeky and fun prospective partner. The sort of happy-go-lucky guy you could take home to your parents and who would entertain your little cousins at family gatherings. In a post-Pennywise and John Wayne Gacy world, though, that all changed. Clowns became sinister and Ronald never recovered. If you see him down a dark alley – avoid. He's angry, crazy, and will most likely try to eviscerate you with a McFlurry spoon.

Murder rating: **7**

Captain Birdseye

He may have kind eyes, but those eyes have seen a lot. The Captain is married to the sea and values marine life above human life. He will lure you on to his boat with seafaring tales then string you up like a big haddock.

Murder rating: **8**

Peperami Animal

All mouth and no trousers. The Animal has had a lot of anger issues during his life, but these are all down to underlying and unresolved family issues. Plus, if you were crammed naked into a salty sleeve you probably wouldn't be particularly affable when you got out, would you? After a few years of therapy I'm happy to report that he is more able to manage his anger and spends much of his time doing crochet and helping less fortunate meat snacks.

Murder rating: **2**

Tony the Tiger

Are you kidding me? The guy is an actual tiger. He will tear your dick off in a second (even if you don't have one).

Murder rating: **9**

Aunt Bessie

While statistically most killers are men, Bessie is the exception that proves the rule. Following in the tradition of Elizabeth Báthory and Mrs Lovett, she is ready to exact revenge on anyone who may have mistreated her, mainly via substandard frozen Yorkshire puddings. There's a reason you never hear about her nieces and nephews.

Murder rating: **10**

Julius Pringle

Yeah, the Pringles guy is called Julius. Initially he seems harmless (he's called Julius and he's just a head), but the moustache is a huge red flag. We're mere months away from someone discovering bodies in his basement. A pile of bodies that have been stacked *perfectly.*

Murder rating: **8**

Snap, Crackle and Pop
Named after what they will do to your bones.

Murder rating: **10**

The Honey Monster
A gentle giant. Only dangerous to diabetics.

Murder rating: **1**

As I've alluded to, the binge eating did not stop after I left university. Like most people, I used to assume life came in distinct phases. You mistakenly believe that each time you segue to a new educational establishment, job or relationship, somehow you will become a new person. This is, of course, total bullshit. No matter what changes around us, the only constant is our own personalities. I know some people will read that as a complete negative. Other people, however, will take that as a complete positive. These people are confident in their own skin and have reached some sort of peace with themselves. They are happy, and should not be trusted. Imagine waking up every morning, stretching and then thinking, 'Oh great! Another day being me!' It's disgusting, really. You should wake up in the morning, have that two to three minutes where you're confused and can't remember who you are or where you are, and then be hit by a crushing wave of reality that you messed up yesterday and you'll probably mess up today as well. I hope that doesn't sound too depressing – it's just being human. Anyone who wakes up and can't wait to 'seize the day' is either a robot or a Peloton instructor.

When I graduated I still assumed these phases existed. After three years of cosseted life at a comfortable university, I decided that the new me was on the way. He was to be a successful man, a ladies' man, a thin man. The issue was, I had no idea how to achieve any of these things. I had spent the last thirty-six months of my life doing the bare minimum on my course (helpfully combined with no actual idea of what I wanted to do with my life), meaning that the 'successful man' element of my transformation wasn't going to be a smooth ride. Even at the time I knew that the ladies' man ambition was unrealistic. I spent my whole university career in a sexual wasteland, which I will cover in a later (very short) chapter about romance. Becoming the 'thin man' was surely the easiest to achieve from this holy triumvirate. I wasn't going to be the triple threat, but surely I could be a single threat?

Well, no. It's all very well to decide the sort of person you want to be, but if you don't actually do anything about it, then it is very unlikely to happen. It's a problem a lot of us have, I think. In my head I was very much the star of a film about my life. I would simply let it happen around me, positive that I was merely in the opening act of an Ed Gamble blockbuster. Sure, everything didn't feel great, but the writers would definitely sort that by the time I hit twenty-five. Now was the time for a montage of me kissing fit girls, working out and being handed wads of cash for an unspecified but highly lucrative job. My montage never quite worked out like that. Wads of cash are a thing of the past for comedians. My actual film would mainly involve me waiting six months for a bank transfer, and when I actually found a fit girl who would kiss me, I would marry her.

So my years after university, food-wise, played out very similarly to the previous three. I did a post-grad in bingeing. I worked hard on my PhD (pretty horrific diet) and I'm oddly proud of it. I would never eat like it now, but I view my past in the same way a reformed football hooligan might look back on his days in the firm. Yes, I had to make a change for my future, but God do I miss the excitement. Compared to a hooligan, though, I was a lot more dedicated to my cause. Most of their high jinks are reserved for a weekend. They get together with their cheeky pals and have a big fight with some other groups of cheeky pals who are wearing different jumpers. Then, come Monday, it's back to their normal lives. I was 24/7.

I was back living in my mum's house and it was immediately as if the last few years hadn't happened – I was straight back to where I was before. Not to say that where I was before was anything other than a privileged and very comfy existence. I was living at home with no real pressure to find immediate employment. There was pressure from my mum, of course, but I didn't consider that real pressure. I was busy – I had full days of eating to schedule, I didn't have time to work. (That said, I am now a judge on *Great British Menu* and writing a book about food, so in many ways I was laying the groundwork back then for an entire career. In your face, Mum.) Days would normally involve waking up late, smoking, watching a box set and then trundling around Raynes Park picking up various lunches that I would load into a plastic bag of joy, take back home and fall into face-first like a clumsy pig. A typical meal would be a panini and some pesto pasta from the Italian deli, two bakes from Greggs, some chips from the kebab shop and dessert from the supermarket (usually a pack of cookies). God, I miss that. Dinner would follow, normally cooked by Mum, and I would dutifully pack down a couple of helpings of that, then it was off out to the pub, which would invariably end with going back to the same kebab shop where I'd bought the chips for my multi-course lunchtime banquet.

I loved Raynes Park Kebab House. Not even necessarily for the food (which was OK, occasionally bordering on adequate). I loved it because they called me 'boss'. I wasn't in a great time of my life career-wise, and this was a taste of what being a high-level exec must be like. I've been reliably informed since that 'boss' is a fairly standard greeting in kebab shops, but honestly it felt different when they said it to me. There was a dewy look to their eyes that seemed to suggest reverence, or at the very least a deep physical attraction. Despite many people claiming that this look was nothing more than the effect of the constant plumes of fatty meat smoke wafting in their eyes, I remain convinced that when they called me 'boss', they meant it. Even if they did call everyone 'boss', I was by far their most regular customer. Without my constant patronage they would've surely gone under. So in many ways I was absolutely their boss and I fully deserved that moniker.

Being a regular at a food establishment is a tricky balance, but the idea of it has always been alluring to me. Walking into my local café or bakery to be greeted by a sing-song 'Morning, Ed! Usual, is it?' sounds like pure heaven. Although in my head I always respond, 'No, I don't think so, Sylvie, I'll be trying something else today!' so I have no idea when I would have established a 'usual'. I'm no creature of habit, who by their nature eat the same things again and again. This is not my style. There are far too many things to try in the world to waste a meal on something you've had before. Despite this, I still like the idea of someone asking me if I want my usual, so perhaps I would have to establish my ever-changing order with Sylvie on my first visit. Sylvie is very accommodating, of course, and would be more than happy to oblige. The only issue would come when Sylvie wasn't working. She can't be expected to work every shift, she's a busy woman. Her dogs aren't going to walk them-selves and her Etsy beret shop is really starting to take off. Best thing for it would be for her to coach the rest of her staff that when I come in, they have to ask me if I want my usual despite me not having a usual and then be prepared to make me a different thing every day. I can't see them toeing that line though (especially Ryan). No, my only option would be somehow to find out Sylvie's shifts and only go to the café/ bakery when she is working. Next thing you know, she gets suspicious that I'm stalking her and I'm doing a ten stretch. It's probably best I don't frequent a local café in that case. In fact, it's probably for the best I don't imagine scenarios any more. They always end up with me doing a ten stretch.

There is a reason I picked a café/bakery for that thought experiment. Those are the ideal places to be a regular. The same coffee and baked goods being part of your regular day is perfectly acceptable. A regular named customer at a sit-down restaurant? No, thank you. That to me suggests either a complete lack of originality or a dark and sad backstory. If I see a man eating alone at a restaurant and conversing with the staff as if he knows them, I assume that either he has no interest in trying new things or his wife has died. If I ever start going to the same restaurant alone night after night and sitting at the same table it will be because I am trying to establish an alibi. Next thing you know, the cops burst through the front door and I'm doing a ten stretch.

I should be more careful when I talk about binge-eating. By any definition that I have found, I was indeed bingeing every day. I would eat no doubt thousands of calories in very short periods of time. And binge-eating is obviously attached to so much more than the calories you're consuming. It's tied to disordered eating and mental health issues, but for the life of me, no matter how hard I try, I cannot consider what I was doing as disordered. I loved it. There was no hesitation at the time, no consideration that what I was doing was bad or in some way compensatory. I simply loved food and wanted as much of it in my body as I could fit in. When I look back on it now, I can of course see that it was unusual behaviour. But all the discomfort with my diet is retrospective. Fat Ed was very happy with what he was up to. He wasn't disordered-eating, he was simply EATING. I've chosen to capitalize that not because I'm angry at you, but because it's the only way to express what I was doing via the medium of text. I was EATING on caps lock. I was wolfing down capitalized meals, and as a result I looked like a capital D in profile. I'm well aware it's probably better for the book if I tell you about a time I was snot-crying into a pie and still ate the whole thing, but I have no stories like that. Having said that, I did once cry because of a pie. It's not the story you trauma-porn muckrakers are slobbering at the thought of, though. I cried because I had dropped the pie and I was really looking forward to eating the pie. To answer the rest of the questions you will have: yes, I did still eat the pie, and it was steak and Stilton.

No matter what you tell people, the majority of the aver-agely weighted public will still insist that fat people have a tragic reason for their body shape. They see a larger person eating a tub of ice cream and assume that their parents must've been killed in front of them by a man dressed as Mr Whippy. So just remember that next time you start pos-tulating about fat people's lives: you're probably wrong, and it's none of your business anyway. I'm not qualified to talk about the issue of fatphobia here, I can only tell you about my perspective when I was in a larger body. I was big because I loved food and I allowed myself to eat whenever and whatever I wanted. That and the bloody male Gamble genetics. There was no Fatman origin story, just a young man with a glint in his eye and a tummy full of chips.

3

AMBER NECTAR AND THE GUINNESS ERECTION

Booze. Tipple. Hooch. Grog. The Hard Stuff. Punch. Moonshine. Giggle Juice. Daddy's Special Water. Snifters. Old Father Timothy's Night-time Medicine. Loosey Goosey Love Liquid. Santa's Lament. These are just a few of the many names we have for alcohol. It's a contentious issue, for sure. Is it a majorly destructive force to the fabric of our society, or an important and beneficial social lubricant? A dangerous elixir that consumes all those who respond to its siren song, or a great contributor to the quality of life and the economy alike? Well, luckily, there's no need to have those debates any more, because I am here to solve it all.

The correct answer is: booze is delicious. That's the end of the conversation. Yes, to some people booze is 'too delicious'. Some people find it so delicious that they have to taste how delicious it is all of the time. So delicious that they have it for breakfast, lunch and tea. I am hopefully not one of those people (I prefer bacon and eggs for breakfast, for example); that's for you to work out over the course of the following pages. In your own heads, I mean. Please don't write to me after you've read this book to diagnose me as an alcoholic. It would really kill the mood of my 11 a.m. Bacardi. The fact is, booze tastes nice and makes me feel fun.

Like most people in the UK, my first encounter with booze came at around the age of thirteen. I say 'like most people' in the desperate hope that this is the case. I haven't really done the research. Research has never been my strong suit; it takes ages and is boring. It may be total nonsense that most children in Britain have their first drink at thirteen, but I did. It might've just been my school, which, looking back, did have a culture of alcohol that was perhaps unusual. You may be one of many sat there reading this, horrified. The idea of a thirteen-year-old drinking does sound insane to me now. I would assume they were part of some sort of pickpocket gang in Victorian London. A down-on-his-luck cheeky chappy who was allowed a nip of brandy on a cold night by his benevolent leader as a reward for a good day's pilfering silk handkerchiefs. This, however, was not the case. It was not Victorian London, it was 1999, and it wasn't brandy, it was Foster's. I wasn't part of a pickpocket gang, having stolen very little in my life. I don't have the constitution for it. My friends and I did once go one by one into a shop with the plan to steal some sweets, but each of us admitted to the others later that we had all panicked and paid for our Freddo bars. Why shouldn't we? That little frog deserved our support.

The first drink I remember having was with my friends. Not in the safe surroundings of a family event, where it can be controlled and overseen by responsible adults and more experienced drinkers, but at an event that was exclusively attended by other total idiots who had never had a drop of alcohol before. It was a voyage of discovery with no captain onboard and a crew that sort of knew how to leave the dock but had no idea how to navigate the ship from then on. We were setting sail for Booze Island but ended up immediately going off course and heading at top speed towards Vomit Straits.

We're often told about the French way of doing things. 'Oh, you know the French will let their kids have wine from a very early age? They will put a few drops of red wine in their water at family meals to acclimatize them.' This is often held up as the gold standard, a way of changing the binge-drinking culture and creating a society of responsible drinkers. Even though it is, let's be honest, totally psychotic. It's micro-dosing with Merlot. Are you supposed to keep increasing the amount of wine in their water bit by bit, so that by the age of twelve they are drinking a bottle of Beaujolais at school dinner? It may make them more comfortable with wine. Surely by that metric, though, it makes them less and less comfortable with water? The pure deliciousness of neat H_2O must surely quickly lose its allure and before long the only creek they will want to drink from is Jacob's. They will be standing at water fountains complaining that the tannins aren't rounded enough. By the time they have a job, they'll be sneaking into the office before everyone else to empty the water cooler and fill it up with a case of the finest Left Bank Bordeaux. Never run a marathon in France. You'll be reaching out for a bottle of Evian, desperate for some much-needed refreshment, and you'll end up with a carafe of Cab Sav. Sometimes, water is enough. On a hot day, there is nothing finer than a tall cool glass of icy water – you want to quench your thirst. The last thing you want to end up with is a fruity and peppery palate.

I'm not one for a Clarkson-style anti-Gallic rant. France is a beautiful country with amazing people, stunning scenery and a food culture that's among the best in the world. All I'm saying is, their children are water-shirking drunks and must be stopped at all costs.

Back to my first drink, which was UK style. None of this café-culture responsibility nonsense. Just good, old-fashioned, wholly irresponsible teenage drinking.

We had planned it for weeks, of course. Talk in school over the previous few months had shifted to the idea of drinking. It's amazing how quickly this sort of thing can happen. We went from Pogs in '96 to yo-yos in '97 to football stickers in '98. Now here we were in 1999 and everybody was talking about drinking beer. I have to admit, it was a shock to me. I was never the one to start these trends at school, merely a gormless and suppliant sheep. I wish I'd had the temerity to stick to my guns and not go with the crowd as a young man, but that wasn't my personality. I was constantly terrified of missing out at school and falling behind my friends, so I went with the tide when it came to drinking, despite being convinced there was at least another year left in yo-yos. Had I not, I would've been a social outcast – a weirdo who spent his lunchbreaks practising a cat's cradle while everyone else shared how much they'd puked that weekend. I would have been a bizarre outsider. Still, think where I would be now! A world champion at yo-yo! Travelling across the globe to demonstrate my nimble and fabulous string-based dexterity. To be fair, this would also have made me a bizarre outsider. It's probably for the best that I lay back and let the booze monster devour me early doors.

The plan was for us all to attend a gig at a nearby church hall. The band in question was a local nu-metal outfit called Kalus. Many of you won't be au fait with the nu-metal trend of the late 1990s/early noughties. I won't go into it too much here; suffice to say it was very interesting and very cool. It was an aggressive form of heavy metal music, often with simplified riffs, torturous lyrics and an occasional white man rapping badly. I loved it, and still do to this day. Practitioners of the art you might have heard of include Korn and Limp Bizkit, bands that are still around now, to the adulation of their fans and the ridicule of many.

The easiest way to spot a nu-metal band is the spelling of their name. You might not have noticed, but both Korn and Limp Bizkit are having some fun with language. 'Korn' is the word 'Corn' except they have cleverly changed the C to a K, as a brave rebellion against traditional crops. Limp Bizkit were having even more of a laugh at orthographical norms. The second word clearly used to be 'biscuit', but by the time Fred Durst and the rest of the Limp lads were done with it, it looked like an explosion at the alphabetti spaghetti factory. In terms of the origin of the name, I suspect it is intended to evoke a lewd act that I'm not going to go into here. In a post-*Bake Off* world, I prefer to imagine 'Limp Biscuit' simply to be something Paul Hollywood might say to a contestant before cruelly refusing to shake their hand.

Kalus (Callous) were firmly in this tradition. Their set was a mix of original material and some old standards (Soulfly's 'Eye For An Eye', etc.) and I was hyped. I had on my baggiest jeans, my sickest Slipknot T-shirt and black eyeliner so badly applied that it looked like I'd been brutally attacked the previous day. Everyone else, though, was more hyped for the drinking. As far as I can recall, we'd simply walked into a shop and bought a pack of Foster's with no hassle. I don't know if that sort of thing is allowed to happen these days, but we experienced very few issues buying beer when we were thirteen. Often, it was left up to me. As one of the tallest and fattest boys in the school it was decided that I was our best hope of being served in corner shops. I suppose the theory was that the shopkeeper would be convinced that nobody could get themselves into my state in just thirteen years on the planet.

I was more than happy to take on the responsibility. I was by no means the most popular boy in school, but you can gain an awful lot of kudos if you're the one who manages to secure the goods. The key was to play it cool. In our teenage brains, we assumed that nobody who goes into a shop to buy beer would walk in, go straight to the fridge, pick up some beers and pay for them. No, that would obviously mark us out as underage scallywags who were up to no good. Instead, I would browse. You know, the way people do in corner shops. I assumed the character of a world-weary nineteen-year-old on his way home from his grown-up job, eager simply to enjoy perusing whatever this particular establishment had to offer. I'd flick through the magazines and newspapers, perhaps raising my eyes to the proprietor, as if to say, 'What's the world become, eh?' I'd pick up a chocolate bar or two, deep in fake thought about which one I should purchase. Which would grace my adult dinner table this evening? 'I like a Boost Guarana, of course,' I'd say with my eyes, 'but the wife likes a Fuse. Chicks, eh!' On one occasion that is particularly painful to remember, I glanced up to the adult magazines on the top shelf, caught the eye of the man behind the counter and said, 'Phwoar.' It went down as well as you might expect.

Only after all this masterful theatre was I ready to make my move. I would amble over to the beer fridge, perhaps whistling or humming to really drive home how casual I was about all of this. I would take it all in. Was tonight a five Foster's for £5 kind of night or was I feeling Kronenbourg levels of flashy? (I was always going to buy the Foster's; this was simply another ruse designed to establish my character.) Then began the slow and relaxed stroll to the counter, my sweaty fingers holding on to the six-pack of Foster's (with one removed) so tightly that my knuckles turned white around the plastic handcuffs that held the cans together. I would plonk the treasure down next to the till, doing my best not to glance out at the increasingly obvious gaggle of excited-looking teenagers, some with their faces pressed up against the glass like they were looking through the window of Hamleys.

'All right, mate?' I would say. All cool, like.

I would then immediately wither under the shopkeeper's gaze before grabbing every other product within reaching distance. Crisps, nuts, chocolate – anything that might suggest I was in fact buying supplies for a sophisticated legal party, rather than a night of teenage debauchery on a public green space. I don't know what sort of high-class dinner-party menu might feature Kinder Eggs and a dust-covered bar of Fry's Orange Cream but it didn't seem to matter. It didn't really occur to me that they couldn't care less and just wanted the custom, but I'm now sure that was the case. I could've been wheeled in on a pram, spat out my dummy and pulled a fiver out of my OshKosh B'gosh dungarees and they still would've sold me a bottle of Glen's Vodka. At the time, though, there was nothing more exciting than pulling off this sort of heist.

It wasn't strictly a heist, I guess. I'd been into a shop and exchanged money for goods. That wouldn't make a great next instalment in the *Ocean's* film franchise. Honestly, though, the rush of adrenalin I experienced whenever I managed to buy booze underage must be comparable to anything Danny Ocean and his rapidly increasing gang of diverse thieves felt post-casino. I'd be welcomed by my pals like a returning war hero. Some hugging me, some high-fiving and the rest desperately pulling at the plastic bag, eager to get the first sip of warm Australian lager. This was all in full view of the shopkeeper, of course. He really did not give two shits.

Now and again we'd stumble into a shop that was run by a stickler for the rules. A law abider. A filthy narc. The sort of guy who would sell you out to the pigs quicker than he could say, 'I'm afraid you have to be eighteen to buy this and I can't sell you the Fry's Orange Cream because it went off in 1991.' In this case, we would revert to plan B: hanging around outside the shop in an attempt to employ the services of a real grown-up who would buy booze for us. The delicate balance to strike was in the selection of the beer mule. This person had to look like enough of a responsible adult to be served by the shopkeeper without question. But also, they must be irresponsible enough to take money from children and go and buy them alcohol. A sixty-year-old vicar? No way was he going to go along with our grand plan, no matter how much we protested that lager was the blood of Christ (this really happened). Plan B rarely worked. People would either turn us down or, as happened on more than one occasion, agree to our terms before taking the money and walking off with it. I respect this option. It's exactly what I would do now.

That night when I first tasted lager, I only had one. I remember being slightly overawed by how disgusting it was. Alcohol was talked about with such reverence by everyone that I assumed it was the most delicious drink in the world. We had been building up to this for months, and the result was that I was now standing in a church hall sipping something that tasted like the bottom of a hamster's cage, except the hamster was dead and the cage was in hell. There were so many things I had drunk up to that point in my life that tasted so much better and I couldn't understand it. Are you telling me that this is what we were all so excited about? Where was this level of enthusiasm for orange squash? Chocolate milkshakes? Even water! I wasn't the most hydrated guy, sure, but even I could taste that a pint of tap water was preferable to alcohol. I wasn't a French kid.

I now found myself at a crossroads. I could vocalize this thought. I could gather all my friends round and say, 'Lads, what are we doing to ourselves? This drink is clearly horrid. There must be another way! Not one year ago we were happy to chug a Capri-Sun and run around for an hour to elevate our minds. Might I suggest we do something similar now? Come on, let's all spin around ten times and fall down on the grass giggling! That will give us the buzz we're so desperately in need of without our mouths tasting like we've licked the bottom of a rusty barbecue. Who's with me?!' Of course, I didn't do that. I wanted to fit in. I suckled on that can of Foster's as if it were the teat of Mother Nature herself. I exclaimed things like 'That hits the spot!' and 'That's a lovely drop!', while exhaling in a way that suggested it was the most refreshing drink I'd ever had. My friends did much the same. I can only assume that they were in an identical position to me – all of us finding this an absolutely disgusting experience, but terrified to be the one to say so for fear of being cast out of the group as a 'pussy' or a 'lightweight'.

This is how it starts. The lie of lager. The first time we have it, we hate it. Then, can by can, pint by pint, we convince ourselves that we love it. 'I'm a beer guy,' we tell ourselves. Eventually we've lied to ourselves so much that our body starts to believe it and the falsehood becomes incontrovertible fact. Nobody in the history of the world has ever liked beer the first time – it's a magic trick we play on ourselves. Brewing is an entire industry built on weak-willed people who want nothing more than to fit in. All it would've taken was the friend of the person who invented beer to speak up. When he was handed that first frothing glass and told, 'Try this, I've been working on it for a while,' all he needed to do was tell the truth. 'Sorry, Harold Beer, this is disgusting. It's a cup of old water. It tastes like you've boiled a load of hay. Whatever you're trying to do here does not work. Let's go and invent lemonade and forget this ever happened.' What a world we would now live in if that had been the case. We'd be able to go and get a pint of Nesquik at our local, and everyone would enjoy themselves and be able to drive home on the motorway fearing nothing more perilous than a weird burp. But Harold Beer's friend didn't say that. He did what we all do: he nodded, and said, 'Delicious.'

That night was an important moment in my life. Not least because it's the only time I've ever had one drink on a night out. Having one alcoholic drink is utterly pointless. Nowadays I will occasionally go out and not have anything to drink, but having one is still a totally bizarre practice in my mind. We've all seen people do it. I say 'people'; I can only assume that they are actually aliens living among us, desperately trying to ingratiate themselves into human society. These aliens, you see, are biologically incapable of processing more than a minuscule amount of alcohol. They will have one for the aesthetic, to put our minds at ease. In their mind, it is much less suspicious to come to the pub and have one drink than it is to have softies all night. But they have not reckoned with me, the alien detective. I am a finely tuned sleuth, machine-tooled to spot these undercover extra-terrestrials. I'm a bit like a Man in Black, except I enjoy wearing colours and I never have a pen on me. If I ever spot anyone stopping at one drink, I simply take them to one side and calmly tell them that it's time to go back to their home planet and report to their squid overlord that the mission has been a failure. This, ironically enough, has caused a lot of people to worry about my drinking, but they'll be thanking me soon enough.

It is much more confusing to me that anyone should have one drink versus nothing at all. There are plenty of legitimate and important reasons why someone would have no alcohol, I'm not here to question that. If you are friends with anyone who would loudly question why someone isn't drinking, cut them out of your life. We have all met these people. They can think of nothing more confrontational than being on a night out and somebody daring not to partake in booze. Listen to the incredulity as they exclaim, 'What do you MEAN you're not drinking?!' They don't even know what the person *means*. They can't even imagine the concept of stepping outside your house without wanting to get lashed. As I said, there are plenty of reasons why somebody might not want to drink. They have a busy day coming up, they're worried about their drinking, or they simply don't want to. They absolutely are not required to explain their actions, of course, but often the only way to get these oafish interrogators off your back is to offer them something. I wish I'd had the courage to stand up to these people in the past, but more often than not I would mumble something about antibiotics and get on with my Diet Coke.

The people who deserve this level of scrutiny are the one-drink people. Having one drink is not self-restraint, it is a pathological red flag. Self-restraint is not having a drink at all and should be admired. Having one drink? What do you MEAN you are having one drink?!

Don't get me wrong, the first drink of a night is wonderful. The warmth, the beginning of the buzz, the feeling of the worries of the day fuzzing round the edges and being washed into the distance by the lapping ocean of sweet booze. The first drink is joyous – it brings perspective, balance and elation. It is, however, only the second-best drink of the night. The main reason for that first drink is so you can have the second drink. That second drink is the best. If the first drink felt like the second drink, I might only have one drink. Powered by the freedom of the first, you are now a brave explorer venturing into denser undergrowth, determined to discover hitherto uncharted delights. The true beauty of the second drink is that it works! Everything you want from alcohol is in that second drink. You become more sociable, funnier, more relaxed. Why would you want to cut short your potential at drink one? That is merely a promise of what is to come, a whisper of the fun you could be having. Having only one drink is like going to the cinema and leaving after the trailers. Yes, we all enjoy the trailers, but think of what you're missing out on.

The window of fun, though, is small. You trick yourself every single time that the third drink will produce the same effect as the second, but it never does. It is diminishing returns from there on. By the time you chase that high into drinks four and five, any increased sociability you gained from drink two has been annihilated into oblivion and you've guaranteed yourself a terrible next twenty-four hours. I will never learn that lesson, though. I always believe that I will one day discover a drink better than that second one. Who knows, maybe I will? For now, I'm happy to put the effort in for the good of mankind.

That night at the Kalus gig, though, I was a one-drink guy. I was happy to see my first beer as an experiment and not an opportunity to get hammered. I came close to having another can, until I saw a friend finish his second and, as the band kicked into a Deftones cover, immediately projectile-vomit on to the wall. You may think that at that moment I felt concern for my friend, but no. I was simply elated that it wasn't me who had been the person to do that. This elation was short-lived as that incident worked out quite nicely for him. He gained the nickname 'Two Cans' and was welcomed as a conquering hero the following Monday.

This was my first taste of the UK's binge-drinking culture. At that age and time, to drink so much that you are violently ill was considered a badge of honour. It's certainly not how my social circle thinks now, and I'm led to believe that young people's attitude to excessive alcohol intake has changed somewhat. Then, however, bingeing was the way to prove to your friends that you were a true adult. I don't know how we got to that point as a country. Being sick is inherently a bad thing. We avoid it at all costs on a daily basis. I literally can't think of anything worse than being sick. So why did it seem to be our aim at least once a week to make our bodies reject everything we had consumed? It wasn't the case with anything else. As a teenager I never once got together with my pals down at the all-you-can-eat Chinese buffet to pound down so much chow mein that one of us chundered on the pavement outside. We never once put on matching polo shirts and went to the Toby Carvery to down jug after jug of gravy while chanting, laughing hysterically if one of us expelled it in a cab on the way home. There is something rotten at the core of alcohol culture in the UK and we never once stopped to question it. We were too busy being sick.

GUINNESS

You may be feeling that I've disparaged beer somewhat. After all, I've claimed that nobody actually likes it and that we are all convinced we do only by Derren Brown-ing ourselves en masse. I should've been clearer: this does not include Guinness. Guinness is the antidote, the salvation.

Many people would claim that Guinness is beer. Guinness is not beer. It is nectar from some unimaginable dark angel, something that as humans we really shouldn't be allowed even to be in the presence of. Every sip of Guinness we take we should (out loud) be thanking whatever glitch in the multiverse is allowing us to taste this liquid black diamond from a utopian alien planet where there is no such thing as pain. What I am trying to say is, I like the taste of it. Not just the taste, but the ritual. The first pour, the tantalizing wait before the second pour. That second pour. The creamy clouds billowing up within the dark, before settling and returning to the blackest black. I can't think of a more enticing image in the entire world of food and drink, perhaps even in the entire world full stop.

When I imagine a pint of Guinness in my head, it is in black and white and in slow motion. I have clearly been heavily influenced by their excellent advertising campaigns and as such probably can't be trusted as a reliable source (I have no idea, for instance, whether the pouring ritual makes any difference to the actual taste of the pint). My mum has always referred to me as an 'advertiser's dream', meaning that I am the absolute target of all marketing. I fall for it every time. As a child especially I was a total mark – any toy that had a fun advert would immediately make me want that product; I almost felt a physical itch. If I ended up getting the toy, though, that would fade fairly quickly. I distinctly remember seeing an advert for a headset-based voice-activated water pistol (the Shout 'n' Shoot 2 from Cap Toys, for fact-heads). The advert featured some kids in a back garden attacking each other with these guns. They would shout 'Fire!' into the microphone, and lo and behold a strong jet of water would burst forth from the barrel. I NEEDED this water pistol.

Firstly, the kids in question were American. This was instant cool points in my mind. Do you remember when something being American made it instantly more attractive? They got films before us, they had cooler trainers, and they didn't say 'pavement', they said 'sidewalk'. Now that the internet has globalized culture, I'm not sure this formula works for today's youth. In the past, if we had a friend who went to America and saw a film that wasn't out in the UK, they would be a hero for at least eighteen months while we patiently waited for it to be released in our cinemas. We had one friend who seemed to go to America all the time and come back with tales of sweets we didn't even know existed, CDs of bands that were the next megastars and fizzy drinks that were bigger than the Empire State Building. We later worked out that he was lying, but only after he also announced that he had been to every country in the world except Luxembourg and had a garage full of mini supercars.

I eventually saved up enough pocket money for the water pistol, and it was a crushing disappointment. I only managed to raise the funds by the time summer was well and truly over, meaning that garden play was limited. Most crucially, I was an only child, and there is only so long that you can stand outside shouting 'Fire!' and spraying water against the wall of the house. It's not like solo play with a tennis ball, something I got quite nifty at. You mainly just take a fair amount of cold splashback to the face, something which tends to snap you out of your futuristic war fantasies and wake you up to the cold reality of what is going on. The strength of the stream was also massively overplayed by the advertisers, meaning that every victorious phrase I shouted into the microphone (such as 'Take a bath!', stolen from the advert, such was my lack of imagination) was followed by a limp and pathetic dribble of water that would drip sadly down my T-shirt. The voice-activation system was also extremely sensitive. The technology wasn't such that it would only fire when I said something sassy and cool ('H_2 oh now you're dead!', 'Take that, wall of house!') but whenever I made any noise whatsoever. Every heavy breath or reassurance to Mum that I would come inside soon would be followed by an underwhelming spurt and the inevitable sprint back into the kitchen to refill the minuscule water tank. It's no wonder we rarely see this system employed in modern warfare.

The fact is, this let-down taught me absolutely no lessons. To this day I am easily swayed by a good bit of marketing and no amount of disappointment will stop me falling for it over and over again. I hope other people are the same. That's how I'm planning on selling this book. You're reading this in the future, so you will know better than me, but the current plan is to push the book with a television ad of some American children reading it in their backyard before screaming, 'Eat my literature!' and tossing it at each other's heads. We have a bestseller on our hands!

Guinness's marketing, of course, is the opposite of the splashy Yankification of 1990s toys. It conjures a peaceful, simple way of life. We are all Irish when we drink Guinness. We are patient, we are poets. We have something to say about the human condition, wry and witty phrases that sum up what it is to exist, all between sips of the black stuff. Even in the middle of a brawl in a London All Bar One on a Saturday night, we are all James Joyce. Even though this is plainly not the case, I still fall for it every time.

I think that's because I believe drinking Guinness is an instant fast track to a personality. It looks so different from all the other pints, I think, it makes me look unique and interesting. I'm not one of these basic commercial lager bitches! I am Ed Gamble! Ed Gamble drinks Guinness! A few years ago, I even fell into the trap of telling people which hostelries do a 'good' pint of Guinness. This is a conversation that pervades Guinness drinking. There are places that do a 'good Guinness' and countless more places that do a 'bad Guinness'. It's a great way of seeming know-ledgeable and thoughtful. You can talk about the lines not being clean and the glass being wrong. I've even parroted the idea that pubs are using the wrong detergent in their glass-washing machines, meaning the foam doesn't cling to the side of the glass in a satisfying enough way. I don't know when in my life I started equating being interesting with being extremely boring, but here we are. That's my personality now. The interestingly boring man. In reality, I'm not sure I hold any of these Guinnpinions (Guinness opinions). I'm simply repeating things that I've heard in pubs or on Guinness YouTube channels that I subscribe to (yes, really).

If I'm in the mood to sound *really* awesome, I'll say that it's impossible to find a good pint of Guinness in the UK. You simply have to go to Ireland, I'll say. This is a line of chat I employed years before I had ever set foot in Ireland. The truth is, I can rarely tell the difference between any pint of Guinness. I like them all. I have my favourite places in London to drink it (the Toucan, Gibney's), but in truth I would happily go into any pub in the UK and enjoy a pint there just as much as anywhere else. I'm not saying that Guinness experts are making it up, simply that I am a heathen and a sheep. In fact, if Guinness started promoting a voice-activated spray-drinking system I would be first in the queue, happily taking myself out to the garden to scream Irish things at walls and then desperately trying to catch drops in my open mouth as they rebounded back to me.

I remember drinking nothing but Guinness for a few years. It was in the fallow period of my life after university and before I started making a living from comedy. I had landed a job at a local pub, the Raynes Park Tavern (RPT), that I absolutely would not have stepped into as a customer. For a start, it was opposite a train station. Nothing good ever happens in pubs opposite train stations. They are the preserve of people who are not in a good place in their lives. They have subconsciously selected a drinking establishment that is close to a means of escape and a method of suicide. More literally, it would often be full of people drinking themselves into oblivion as soon as they had alighted from the train after work, and this did not create a happy vibe. Scores of men with slightly loosened ties putting off the inevitable return to their homes, hoping that a few cheap jars would soften the blow of what was clearly a life they were not content with.

It was also surprisingly dangerous for the area. Raynes Park is just down the road from Wimbledon, which of course is a leafy and comfortable part of London populated by well-to-do mums whiling away their days in Côte Brasseries and emotionally ignoring their children. Raynes Park may be near by, but has still managed to remain Wimbledon's slightly unpredictable cousin. The RPT was the heart of this vibe. On more than one occasion when I arrived for work there was an ambulance parked outside. Not, I hasten to add, because the paramedics were inside having a quick half. (Not that I would begrudge them that. They work hard and they, more than anyone, deserve a bit of a settler halfway through a shift.) No, it was there as a result of fights that had ended badly. One night I arrived for work and literally had to step over a pool of blood outside the door. Initially I assumed someone had dropped a glass of red wine on the steps, but upon entering I was informed that one of the regulars had battered one of the other regulars after he said something disparaging to his girlfriend. Such was the tightness of the community in the RPT, the police were not involved and both regulars remained regulars for the rest of my tenure there, simply drinking slightly further away from each other after that. There's a lot to be said for a pub as a community space, but people tend to forget that a lot of communities are populated by some total nightmares.

Thanks to the draw of alcohol, though, I soon became part of this Raynes Park community. I started drinking in the pub on my nights off. I absolutely cannot recommend this if you work in a pub. It really doesn't feel like you're winning at life if you end up drunk in the place where you work. You believe that you've made some friends, but really you are just united by booze. These are 'friendships' that are based entirely on conversations you can't remember with people you would not spend time with sober. My best friend in the pub was a man in his late forties who wore rings on every finger. The bar manager told me she thought he took a ring from every person he killed, but I chose not to see this as a red flag because he was always very generous with tips and free drinks. One morning he dropped by to give me a tracksuit that didn't fit him. I had apparently agreed to this donation the previous evening when I'd popped in for a few on my night off, but I had no memory of this. My mum hid it well, but I think this is the most she has ever worried about where my life was going. Nothing prepares you as a parent for your child coming back from his job with a big grey tracksuit that a middle-aged man has given him for no discernible reason. I left the job in the pub soon after this, which was lucky. That guy might've got himself a new ring.

I drank so much Guinness in the year I worked there that Mum was probably right to be worried. We would occasionally have lock-ins and I remember the landlord commenting that I drank Guinness 'like it was water'. If you take into account that the landlord was a massive Irishman, this was cause for concern. Some nights after my shift I would spend my entire wage packet for that evening on pints, which is not only spicy behaviour but also completely negates the point of having a job in the first place.

Nowadays, I have a much healthier relationship with the black stuff. Some of you might disagree. You might suggest that someone writing a lengthy section dedicated to one drink is rather obsessive. You might have a point, but I'm nowhere near where I was in what I'm choosing to refer to as the Black Summer of 2008.

Every now and then I have a Guinness Foreign Export. I can't say I hugely recommend it. At a hefty 7 per cent it will send you to space before bringing you back into Earth's atmosphere with a violent thump. It has all the flavour profile of Guinness as you know it, but without the alluring creaminess, meaning it feels like you are drinking some sort of Victorian medicine they would've given to women to stop them being so bally hysterical.

The first time I had it, I was not aware of the strength. I wasn't really aware of different strengths of alcohol at all, if I'm honest. I would drink anything presented to me at the same speed (quickly) and in the same volume (loads). I would of course find myself much drunker on stronger drinks, but I never made the connection and simply assumed it to be a randomized system. My dad and I both fell for this when we were on holiday. I was sixteen, which is an acceptable age to start drinking with your dad (unless you're French, in which case this is a decade too late). We were at a pizza restaurant for lunch and decided to order a bucket of eight Foreign Exports. A bold move at lunch, granted. Dad then regaled me with facts, as dads love to do. This drink, he told me, was exported primarily to the Caribbean and West Africa, where it was marketed as a sexual boost for men worried about impotence. I can't verify this, but I do know that huge amounts of strong alcohol traditionally have the opposite effect. It certainly didn't affect my libido at that lunch because I was drunk, and more importantly with my father.

After just one bottle, everything got a bit fuzzy. I remember being distinctly embarrassed that I was drunk so quickly. I'm not someone who has always been desperate to impress his dad, but this felt like I'd let him down somewhat. He had a pathetic weak son who got tipsy after only one beer. However, as per my golden rule of two drinks plus, I had to have another. This was before the pizza arrived, and I felt things sharply go off the rails. What latent shame I had was washed away by a tsunami of booze and I was soon acting the giddy goat. Thinking that it might make him laugh, I slipped off the label from one of the bottles and stuck it to my forehead. I looked up at him for the big reveal, and much to my surprise he had done *exactly the same thing*. While I had been in my head about what ridiculous drunken thing to do next, he had been going through the exact same thought process. There's never been any doubt about my parentage, but if I ever needed any confirmation that this man was definitely my biological father, this was it. It was like looking in a mirror. Two idiotic and drunk men, both with Guinness labels in the centre of their ample foreheads. We broke down into fits of laughter.

Consider this the best advert for Foreign Export you will ever find. The only drink (as far as I'm aware) that will increase the strength of your erection as well as bring you closer to your dad.

4

SPIRIT GUIDE

It is fairly likely that if you know one of the 'What do you MEAN you're not drinking?!' people that you will also know a 'SHOTS!' person. Because they are the same people. This is true one hundred per cent of the time – it's an immutable scientific fact. Even at the quietest and tamest night at the pub, they will declare that it is time for everyone to do shots, regardless of whether you actually want to or not. In fact, they genuinely prefer it when you don't want to. Any resistance they're met with causes their eyes to light up, delighted with the thrill of the chase. The most satisfying result for these people is getting the person who definitely didn't want to do a shot to do a shot, ideally followed by a pained and disgusted face. Even better if they have an actual reason to not want to. The holy grail for these people would be getting a pregnant recovering alcoholic who has her car with her to do a shot. You can try and deny them when they initially ask, but this does no good. They will go through the motions of asking who wants a shot, but this means nothing. Say there are ten people at the table. Firstly, congratulations on being so popular. Secondly, imagine that six people say yes, they would like to have a horrible tiny drink. This survey they have just done is a sham. They are coming back from the bar with ten shots.

Ninety per cent of the time, it is tequila. I've since discovered that nice tequila exists and is a joy. In those early years of drinking though, I hated tequila. The first time, I remember being convinced I was being pranked and someone had gone to the cleaning cupboard and poured me a measure of bleach. Not even one of the fancy flavoured bleaches – a plain bleach. Any drink where part of the ritual is eating salt and sucking a lemon should not legally be allowed to be a drink. But this is what characterizes shots and drinking as a whole when you are a younger person: it's never about anything tasting nice, it's about getting as drunk as possible as quickly as possible – and for some people it's about the sadistic pleasure of seeing people they claim to love in agony.

I'm not saying I didn't get involved in all of this. As you know by now, I was a total sheep. If my friends told me something was what everyone had to do, I did it. Looking back, I really should've listened to my logic and my heart more. When I say 'logic' and 'heart', I mean my mum. She was always concerned about my drinking at such a young age, while simultaneously realizing there was little she could do. All she could offer was advice about not going with the crowd. Time and time again she would utter the sentence, 'If all your friends jumped off a cliff, you would as well, would you?'

This is a very unfair hypothetical situation to offer a teenager. Mum was never able to back it up with more context, no matter how much I requested it. Why were we at a cliff? Why would they all jump off? Do they say anything before they do it? Are they wearing any safety equipment? If all my friends suddenly and for no reason jumped off a cliff, the chances are that, no, I would not join them. Even if they pleaded with me to follow them, I like to think I would be strong enough not to go ahead and plunge to my death. If they were abseiling, though, I would be there in a heartbeat. If they were all jumping into the sea and there were girls watching, I'd be first off the edge. If they were filming a cool *Jackass*-style video, just you try and stop me. In fact, I can think of far more instances where I would have followed my friends off a cliff at that age than ones where I'd remain at the top. Of course, I never said this to Mum. I would reply, 'No, of course not, I am my own man – I do what I feel is right in my heart.' Not true. Certainly not when it came to alcohol. Any disgusting concoction that came my way was going straight down my throat without my even stopping to ask what it was.

This included tequila. After that it was an arms race to discover shots that were even more punishing and dangerous and turned drinking into an extreme sport. The internet was flourishing at this point and provided a bible of totally idiotic ways to consume alcohol that would, yes, get us hammered, but also make us feel like totally radical hard men. Allow me to present a few recipes for the most unnec-essarily dangerous and disgusting drinks you could possibly consume.

SUICIDE TEQUILA

Ingredients
Cheap tequila
Table salt
Lemon wedge
Nose
Mouth
Eye

We dabbled for a while in Suicide Tequilas. It wasn't quite what it sounds like, although I wouldn't put it past us that we might've tried a drink where you had to neck a shot and then immediately take your own life. No, this was worse. As if licking salt, drinking tequila and sucking a lemon wasn't bad enough, the suicide variation switched it up. You had to snort the salt, drink the tequila and finish things off by squirting the lemon in your eye. It baffles me that the drinking of the tequila is the only constant across the different disciplines. You go to all that effort to up the stakes and you leave the traditional method of drinking the same? Pathetic. Why not eat the shot glass? Suck the tequila up your butt? Pour it directly into the charging port of your phone, at least. If you're insisting on punishing yourself for having a nice time, let's really go for it!

I only tried the Suicide Tequila once, but it felt too ridiculous even for me. My rule now is not to drink anything at the end of the night that you wouldn't drink at the start. If you met someone in a bar at 7 p.m. and their first drink involved them snorting salt and squeezing lemon in their eye, you would delete them from your phonebook and call a hospital. This should not change just because it's 3 a.m. This stands for anyone ending a night out with something they would drink at the start of the day. I once saw someone order a glass of milk in a Wetherspoons. I can only assume that man was either a time-travelling Victorian or a *Batman* villain. Avoid these people at all costs.

THE STATUE OF LIBERTY

Ingredients
Sambuca
Lighter
Finger

The Statue of Liberty features tequila's binge-drinking cousin, sambuca. Apart from combining everyone's least favourite flavour, liquorice, with a syrup the consistency of phlegm, sambuca has another interesting property: it is flammable. The Statue of Liberty was imbibed thusly. The consumer would dip their finger into a shot of sambuca and then light it. Acting quickly (there's only a second or so before the flame starts hurting), they then hold their fiery digit aloft and down the rest of the shot before quickly sticking the finger in their mouth to soothe the burn. As far as I'm aware, this doesn't exactly capture the spirit of what the Statue of Liberty is supposed to stand for. When the boats of immigrants entered the waters around New York City, they told tales of seeing the statue and being filled with excitement about everything she represented for their new start in the land of hope and the American Dream. At no point did they lay eyes on Liberty Island and look forward to being greeted by a painful and flaming drunken mess (although this is perhaps more realistic).

The first time I tried the Statue of Liberty was the last time I tried the Statue of Liberty. I've never been one for being able to remember a series of instructions in a row and this was no exception. Lighting my finger was no issue, it went up like a birthday candle. At that point, though, I went into sheer panic mode and the order of everything else went out of my head. It was only my friends screaming 'Drink it!' that reminded me of the main step in the process. I held my finger in the air and did as instructed. The next bit of the ritual was the most important. It is key that you get your finger in your gob as quickly as possible to reduce the damage the burning booze is inflicting on your flesh, but this is the one step that evaded me. For reasons completely unknown to me, I attempted to cool my blazing finger by dunking it in the nearest wet place I could think of. Unfortunately, this was the empty shot glass. I say 'empty': there was enough sambuca residue still inside. And if there's one thing we know about sambuca? It's flammable. I introduced the naked flame on my naked flesh back into the very liquid that had helped light it in the first place. I created what can only be described as a mini fireball, burning my finger to such an extent that I had to wear a plaster for a week. I wish I could say this gained me some sort of legendary status, but sadly not. The assembled throng simply dispersed after the initial fireworks, leaving me to find a tap to run my injured digit under. No nickname, no plaudits. Fair enough. It wasn't like I'd been sick.

THE FLAMING LAMBORGHINI

Ingredients
Sambuca
Kahlúa
Baileys Irish Cream
Blue curaçao
Icing sugar?
Straw

This might be the most dangerous cocktail on the list. Quite why I ever thought it was a good idea is beyond me, but I'm sad to report it was probably down to my pathetic notion of masculinity evidenced by my fascination with open flames. I've been worryingly obsessed with fire since I was a child. If I was to describe my perfect evening it would probably be 75 per cent me staring into a raging furnace. Even now, when I do a barbecue I will stand and gaze into the coals and go somewhere else in my brain. My wife caught me doing this once and I swear it's the most she's ever looked like she was on the verge of leaving me. At least a barbecue is somewhere that is predisposed to flames, so it was a graduation from where I used to be. As a child I once set fire to the toilet roll while it was still on the wall holder. It was an interesting practical demonstration of science. Because of the air pockets in between the sheets, it went up quickly and spectacularly, scorching the wall and creating a gigantic plume of smoke. I wish I could say that when I apologized to my mum I meant it, but I didn't. It delighted me.

So, when I arrived at university as a rotten-faced fresher, I was immediately intrigued by the Flaming Lamborghini. For the fire aspect, yes, but also because of the theatrical and interactive elements. The way it works (certainly in my then local cocktail bar) is this. Into a large fishbowl-type vessel, the bartender poured a mix of Kahlúa, Baileys and blue curaçao. This in itself would be a perfectly delicious cocktail to drink without the fear of immediate self-immolation. But that's not what we were after. We wanted a drink, yes, but we also wanted the threat of ending up like the guy on the cover of the first Rage Against the Machine album. As you started drinking this with a straw, the bartender would pour in (from a great height) flaming shots of our old pal sambuca and any other flammable spirit they could lay their hands on. As a customer, you were now drinking from a giant fireball. The bartender would keep pouring in fiery liquids before also sprinkling in some sort of powder which was somehow more flammable than everything else. To this day I have no idea what that powder was. Icing sugar? Gunpowder? Talc? Whatever it was, all it added to the drink was yet more red crosses to the bar's health-and-safety assessment.

Some things to be taken into account. The bar we used to do these in was not a clean workspace. The bar itself would be covered in pools of alcohol from the last group to do a Flimbo Limbo (I was drinking them so regularly I had to shorten the name). These pools would, of course, routinely ignite as the bartender splashed literal fire all over the place. The main issue, though, was the straw. On more than one occasion the plastic straw provided would melt in the drink WHILE YOU WERE DRINKING IT. Not only would you be gleefully consuming a week's worth of units and actual flames, there was a high chance you would also swallow molten plastic and toxic fumes. These days we are encouraged to use paper straws to save the environment. This is a notion I am of course onboard with, except when it comes to the Flimbo Limbo. I pray to Jesus every night that that cocktail bar has not awoken to the climate crisis. Can you imagine the carnage of a paper straw in that hellmouth of a drink? It would go up quicker than a toilet roll on a loo wall. You go into a bar for a jazzy drink and next thing you know your noggin is engulfed. And please don't talk to me about metal straws. They may seem like the best option in this scenario, but think of the conductivity! That straw would heat up to the temperature of an iron within seconds and you'd be left with a brand on your hand like a human cow.

Plus, this is clearly not the best option in this scenario.

The best option in this scenario is not to have a drink that could double as a daredevil act from Zippos Circus. Imagine if this drink went as disastrously wrong as it could go. You'd end up with terrible burns all over you and you'd have to spend the rest of your life explaining that, no, you are not a war veteran, you sustained these injuries thanks to a Flaming Lamborghini. You would then have to clarify that, no, you weren't in a horrible accident involving a supercar. You did in fact willingly allow a bartender (who I'm assuming would not have been a certificated fire marshal) to pour burning liquid into a bowl centimetres from your face with the express intention of swallowing said burning liquid. You'd be laughed out of the burns unit. Next thing you know, you've internalized all that bitter rage and after many years of secluding yourself from society you decide to take out all your anger on the good people of Gotham. From there it's a slippery slope to ordering milk at a Wetherspoons.

All of these drinks of course come with a heavy 'please don't try this at home' warning. In fact, please don't try them *anywhere*. If you have the facilities, equipment and inclination even to attempt a Flaming Lamborghini at home, you have other issues we need to discuss. That being said, there is clearly a huge market for dangerous drinks. And if there's a market, I want to be involved.

So now I am very excited to present a brand-new cocktail from my own brain: Thor's Hammer. I believe it to be the most dangerous and exhilarating drink available. I am not liable for any risk to health, I simply expect to make a bucket of cash from it in the coming years.

THOR'S HAMMER

Ingredients

Brandy
Rum
Sambuca
Vodka
Rubbing alcohol
Official Ed Gamble Asbestos Hammer
(available from my website at
£125.99)
Fresh mango

Method

Mix all of the flammable liquids in a bucket, before setting them alight with a match. Proceed to drink the entire contents of the bucket by dipping in the Official Ed Gamble Asbestos Hammer (which will itself be on fire) and licking the concoction off drip by drip. Once you have finished the drink (assuming you have not perished), take aim and throw the hammer at the biggest man in the bar (even better if he is working security). Once he approaches to pummel you, bribe him with the fresh mango.

If you still need convincing, perhaps I should take some advice from the gin marketing board. Those guys have gone into overdrive in the last decade. Once the preserve of the true drunk, even gaining the nickname 'Mother's Ruin', gin has had a glow-up. It's now considered one of the most refined spirits, no longer something someone might make in a bathtub in a grimy London borough during the plague. A better nickname for it now might be 'Mother's Christmas Present' given the obsession advertisers have with marketing it to women of a certain age.

With the continual gin-washing we have been experiencing came the birth of reprehensible and twee gin-based slogans and accompanying merch. We've all seen this stuff – a tea towel emblazoned with 'Let the Fun Be Gin' or a piece of driftwood with 'It's Gin o'Clock' crudely daubed on it. Anyone who has any of these things in their house should be thrown in jail for being first-degree basic. I obviously don't mean that. I mean they should be killed, but until our government brings back the death penalty specifically for purchasing awful tat, I'll have to insist that prison time is the only option.

It also annoys me that of all the alcoholic drinks, gin has been chosen as the focus of this unremitting faecal tidal wave of trinkets. Sure, prosecco gets a look in now and again (e.g. 'Save Water, Drink Prosecco'), but the majority of these slogans tend to centre on gin. Think of all the different options that are being left on the table! Never one to miss an opportunity, here are some of my suggestions for fun and hilarious alcohol-based landfill for your horrible house:

An apron that says 'Live, Laugh, Polish Lager'.

A tote bag featuring the sentence 'Don't talk to me until I've had my secret vodka that I keep in my child's nappy bag'.

A mug design that clearly states 'Keep Calm and Drink Espresso Martinis (Good Luck)'.

A framed print (curly font) that says 'This house runs on anger and Stella Artois'.

Head bandages embroidered with 'No, I'm not a veteran, I had an accident with a Flaming Lamborghini'.

OK, I'll keep working on it. The truth is, I'm not much of a spirits guy . . .

5

THIN BASTARD

Given that I was perfectly happy in my larger days, people often ask me why I chose to try and lose weight. Truthfully, while I was fine with my size and actively liked eating huge piles of food, I didn't *feel* great. By feeling great, I mean physically rather than emotionally. I had yet to realize that there was a link between the two, but made the decision, aged twenty-three, that it might be nice to get a bit fitter and gain some more energy.

I had also been booked for one of my first television performances on *Russell Howard's Good News*. I thought it might be nice to try and drop a bit of weight to feel fresh for the show, as at that point I was at my heaviest after letting everything really get out of control. People often tell me I never looked my nineteen stone, but I certainly felt it. Although I've crowed about being happy, I suppose vanity did play a part in my decision to cut some pounds. I wanted to go on television and look slim, and I'm sorry. It's not like there was any pressure on me to lose weight for the show, it was my own desperation to be seen as attractive that led me down this path. This was comedy, not modelling. Comedy is much more relaxed about how you look. There's no evil agent behind the scenes, measuring your waist and weighing you every week. 'Oh, you want to play the Lowestoft Chuckle Hut, do you? Well, you'd better start eating cotton wool, because they are very specific about the sort of look they want.' As long as you're funny, you can gain some recognition in the industry. As a caveat, I will say that this perspective is coming from a male cis comic. The pressure of looking right for non-male comics is still huge, but for me, even if I'd turned up to gigs in a tracksuit covered in mustard I still would've been given the benefit of the doubt.

Making fun of your perceived flaws is also actively encouraged. Comedy is one of the only disciplines that welcomes that. If you were an undertaker who kept putting the wrong bodies in the coffins, you couldn't make that your 'thing'. Nobody would entrust Oopsie Daisy & Sons to take care of their departed loved ones, regardless of how funny they are about their mistakes. With stand-up, the last thing people want to hear from an anecdotal comedian is what you're proud of and how well you're doing. They want to hear about your life going wrong, the times you've failed (with hilarious consequences). This is especially true of British audiences. They come to comedy gigs for a good time. The last thing that is a good time for a Brit is hearing that someone's life is on track. That's not comedy – that's a stark and harsh reminder of everything that's wrong in your own life. Any sign that you are proud or smug about your life will immediately turn a British audience against you. Here, I've imagined the worst possible opening lines for a comedian in the UK.

Hey guys, hope you're having a good night! I know I am! Because all my nights are good! I'm very happy in my personal life, I have a rock-solid marriage and I'm in great shape. How crazy is it when everything is so great?! It's like, I don't think anyone has ever been this fortunate! Anyway, who's drinking? I'm not – it slows down my productivity – but you guys do you, yeah?

They would be chased out of the venue and killed. Because there is absolutely no humour in things going well. In America, things are different. They welcome self-improvement and are in awe of people striving to achieve their dreams. Comedy audiences are enthusiastic (sometimes too enthusiastic) and will whoop and cheer things that a British audience would grumble and sneer at.

When I lost weight, I decided I had to do material about it. It was, after all, a drastic change in my life. Surely I could get something out of it? I had not taken into account how difficult it would be to talk to a British audience about it though. 'We are British,' they would say with their eyes, 'we don't want to hear about this.' When I did this material in America, they would lose their minds. I would mention how many pounds I had dropped, and they would screech with encouragement so much that it eventually became quite annoying. I longed for the British reaction of 'I bet you were funnier when you were fat, you prick!'

You see, being fat as a comic was my thing. The old adage goes 'Write what you know,' and I knew being fat. As such, it made up a lot of my material in the noughties. I would talk about injecting insulin as a fat person in public ('It looks like I'm trying to pop myself') and almost everything I said played into the funny fat man persona that I had established at school. (I was injecting insulin because I am type 1 diabetic, by the way, not just for fun. And if you think that's the last time that's being mentioned, then you are absolutely kidding yourself.) Perhaps this is also something that made me feel uncomfortable. This had been my whole life up until this point. I had used humour at school to high-light my differences and protect myself from the mean comments I assumed people would be making. This takes its toll. Rather than leaving all that behind after education, though, I had literally made it my job. Walking out in front of audiences and making fat jokes about myself before any of them shouted any. It felt like it was time for a change.

Plus, and I can't stress this enough, I was vain and wanted to fit into clothes from River Island.

THE 'SECRET'

When I started to lose weight, the most regular question I got was 'What's your secret?' People would ask me that all the time. It's probably something I'd asked in the past. What an odd turn of phrase that seems to have infiltrated its way into our lexicon surrounding matters of health and weight – 'secret'. When you think about it, this is very dramatic vocabulary for something so mundane. Secrets are normally reserved for soap operas and magicians. It suggests that everyone who has lost weight has automatically signed up to some sort of clandestine society, where they are bound by rules of silence. As if we step on the scales, see we have lost a few pounds and then the scales start speaking to us: 'You are now part of the Skinny Circle. You must not reveal any of your weight-loss secrets, under pain of DEATH.'

This question is often asked with the urgency of someone who thinks there is actually a secret. When I told them my 'secret', they were often disappointed and refused to accept the answer. The answer for me was eating less and starting to exercise. This has got to be the most boring secret of all time. For a start, it is not a secret, nor has it ever been a secret. This is, on paper, the only way to successfully lose weight long term. But this is not what people want to hear. They want an actual secret. What they wanted me to say was 'Eat pineapple before 6 a.m.' or 'Start walking with your feet turned out like a duck,' but I had nothing like that to offer them. All I could say was 'Eat less, exercise more.' Now and again, if I was bored, I would give them something juicy like 'When I was eleven I killed my babysitter,' but then I'd have to clarify that this was more of a general secret that had very little to do with weight loss. I should probably tell you now that I did not kill a babysitter, but amazingly this is something they didn't follow up on, so eager were they for health tips from a man who had only very recently lost a few stone.

Then again, I'd imagine that murdering someone might actually be a good way to lose weight. If I had actually killed someone, I probably wouldn't fancy eating very often. The stress would affect my appetite, and all the digging would have been a good load of cardio. I'm not recommending this to anyone, but letting your guilt consume you is probably a very effective diet. Plus, if you get caught, the restrictive prison diet would probably do wonders. With the diet industry the way it is, I think we are less than a year away from some influencers promoting a prison-diet programme.

Hi guys! A lot of you have been asking for my secret to weight loss and I'm very happy to reveal it to you today. I've been working with the brilliant people at HMP Wormwood Scrubs and together we've come up with the ultimate health and lifestyle plan to get you in shape for the summer! It's called Locked Up, Jacked Up, and for just £30 a month, you can join the revolution!

For your money you will get . . .

Your own prison canteen-style segmented tray to act as a portion guide!

Daily deliveries of poorly subsidized meals!

Access to our exclusive workout yard for an hour a day! (Form your own intimidating gang to get more time on the bench press!)

A loud and intrusive wake-up call every morning!

Monthly catch-up sessions with our trainers from behind glass using a little telephone!

And for just £50 extra a month, we will provide you with a burly man with a tattooed face to smack every other meal out of your hands!

The sad fact is, there is no secret. I lost weight the boring way that we are always told works. I started eating less, and more nutritiously, and I started exercising. If you've come to this book for some sort of revelation, I'm afraid this is where I let you down.

THE 'DIET'

Once they'd dispensed with the fact that there is no secret, everyone was always concerned with what diet I went on. Was it Atkins? Did I use WeightWatchers or LighterLife or Locked Up, Jacked Up? I'm afraid I'm about to disappoint you again. Yes, I had tried diets in the past in acts of desperation. They never worked. Because by definition they are temporary and drastic changes to your lifestyle that never last. You may get some initial amazing results, but as soon as you return to what you were doing before, everything goes back to the way it was. This has been terrible for my mental health. I apply all my willpower to losing weight by being hungry all of the time and fantasizing about all the foods I miss, only for that to collapse. I'm then left with no results and on top of that hating myself for what I perceive to be my weak will. Unless it's sustainable long term, I found, there's no point doing it. Even using the term 'diet' feels mad. A diet is literally just whatever you are eating on a day-to-day basis. We are all on a diet, regardless of what we are eating. If you aren't on a diet, you are dead. Your diet should just be what you can maintain for the most part – food that you enjoy and makes you feel nice and that you can persevere with. If you are tempted suddenly to change what you are eating for a short intense period of time, I can't recommend it. It will make you feel worse physically in the short term and then worse mentally long term when you inevitably return to old habits.

I can't apologize for this enough, but losing weight for me in the first instance was actually quite easy. I didn't go on any official diet or follow any exercise programme. I didn't cut out carbs or eat exclusively beef or start doing hot yoga. Because I was already in the worst shape I could possibly be. I was eating mountains of food and never moving my body. So, all I needed to do was live a more normal lifestyle. Granted, not much of a marketable diet. I can't see myself on posters promoting the benefits of one lunch instead of two, or making a loaf of bread last two days rather than twelve minutes. It was small changes that had a big impact. That's the only tip I have for losing weight. Get yourself into the worst state you can possibly imagine and then even slight tweaks will melt the fat off you.

Gone was the big daily lunch crawl. Multiple pastries were replaced with a single pastry, two sandwiches were replaced with one sandwich. I went on a normal-person diet. The sort of diet that the average person complaining about their weight and going on a diet would be eating. The results came fairly quickly – but the key was, I could maintain this. I wasn't really avoiding things I liked, I was just eating less of them. Not much of a secret, is it? Most diets will tell you to throw out all your biscuits, and never let them cross your lips again. Mine would tell you to eat only six rather than twelve. Perhaps that's the only advantage of being truly, hugely overweight.

People started to notice that my clothes were getting a bit looser, and I started to look a bit thinner in the face. As I've already mentioned, this led to many questions about my 'secret'. There were some who went with a slightly more problematic line of questioning, however.

ARE YOU ILL?

Unbelievably, this is a question I got on a regular basis while I was losing weight. Are. You. Ill? Imagine asking that to someone. What a risky opening gambit. You see that someone has lost weight and decide the best thing to do is openly check if they have a disease that has the side-effect of reduced appetite. The first time I heard it, it made me laugh out loud. I couldn't believe the audacity of the question. What are you trying to get across to someone? You want to tell them that you've spotted that their body shape has changed, but also you want to let them know that it doesn't look nice. That they look unwell and you are worried about them.

To be fair, I've often found that the best way to deal with someone who you think might be ill is to just ask them outright. Don't wait for them to tell you, just say it! You can't be hanging around, conversing with someone and *hoping* that they'll let you into their intimate lives. You don't have the time! You have lots of friends and family to subliminally insult. Just get the question out the way! Same goes for if someone looks tired. Before they've had a chance to tell you anything, just say, 'You look tired.' I love it when people do that, because it lets you know immediately that you look like a haggard old fart. Then you can go about your day knowing that you look like a haggard old fart and that everyone you meet probably thinks the same.

My favourite people of those who asked me if I was ill were the ones who immediately realized their mistake after I explained that, no, I was just trying to lose some weight. That would hang in the air, and their faces would change. They would slowly realize (very slowly . . . these often weren't the sharpest minds) that they had essentially just insulted me. They would then desperately try to backtrack and say, 'Well done, you look great actually!' This is quite the about-turn. From 'You look ill' to 'You look great!' I hope to God none of them were medical professionals. They would spend their nights running up to people in A&E saying, 'God, you look awful, we have to see to you immediately,' before discovering that they were actually talking to someone who has brought an injured person in to be seen. They'd then panic and backtrack, spending far too much time telling them how wonderful they looked while the ill person perished.

Perhaps these people were in fact being cautious. Maybe they used to be the sort of person who told those who had visually lost weight that they looked great. Then one day, it backfired. They told their friend that they looked amazing only to find out that their friend had worms. Or maybe they asked someone their secret, only to be told that the secret was bereavement. So, they changed their technique. Now they assumed the worst, to save themselves from embarrassment. Then they found that asking someone if they're ill is potentially much more embarrassing. What are they to do?

I have a suggestion. How about – and this will blow your minds – don't mention it at all? Much is made of the positives of talking openly in this day and age. We have to talk, people say. Ask your friends if they're OK! In many instances, this *is* a positive thing to do. I do worry, though, that we have lost the beautiful art of shutting up and minding our own business. The situation I have been describing is the perfect opportunity to practise shutting up and minding your own business. If you see someone for the first time in a while and their body shape has changed in whatever way, simply don't mention it. Talk to them about other stuff. Don't take the risk of establishing whether it is for positive or negative reasons, just be quiet. If, during the course of the conversation, they offer you some information about it, talk to them. Congratulate them if they are happy about it or listen to them if they are worried. But please, never instigate. It's not your body, you see. If it was, you'd be perfectly welcome to ask yourself if you are ill or say you look nice, but then the person you're with might be concerned. In this instance, they are allowed to ask you if you're ill.

BEFORE AND AFTER

I lost about seven stone all told in that initial burst of a year. Visually, the results (I'm told) were quite startling. People who hadn't seen me for a while were shocked, to say the least. This usually led to them blurting out something like 'Oh my God, you're actually really handsome!' I'm willing to accept that if they had been given a moment to compose what they were going to say in their heads before letting rip with it, they might have phrased it differently. My preference in this situation, as I've said, is that people say nothing, just to be on the safe side. But I can see how shock played a role. I looked quite different. 'You're actually really handsome' wasn't necessarily my favourite thing to be told though. You start retracing all of your past meetings with these people and imagining their inner monologue. *He's quite ugly*, they must've been thinking. Or worse, *He could really look nice if he didn't look like this*. At the time I was bigger, I certainly didn't think I looked bad. I still don't think I did. I could've probably looked after myself a bit better, sure. Worn nicer clothes, washed my hair more, not happily gone out with mustard on me. But I was a man in his early twenties. I was dishevelled, as a lot of them are.

When a thin man is dishevelled and a bit dirty, people seem to think they have a certain allure. A grimy rock 'n' roll edge. Add a few stone to the man, however, and he is just a mess. This was the era of indie sleaze. Everyone seemed to love bands that featured wiry men who looked like they hadn't showered or slept in a week, with hair like an exploded thatched roof. They were adored. Girls fancied them. They were dangerous. But let me tell you, this adoration stopped if the man in question was nineteen stone.

This is a double standard we don't talk about enough. It's all very well saying that you are attracted to men who look like they don't take care of themselves, but you have to be consistent. I wasn't looking after myself at all and I committed to it far more than those indie rockers. I was dangerous, but just because the danger I posed was mainly to my blood cholesterol levels, I wasn't considered in the same sexy category as Pete Doherty. I had all of the indie sleaze attributes going for me. A big shock of messy hair, crumpled clothes and bags under my eyes. I couldn't quite pull off the skinny jeans, so instead opted for bootcut jeans that trailed on the floor. They trailed on the floor because no jean makers can countenance the idea that someone with my waist size (I hit a peak of forty-two inches) would not also be seven feet tall. I did all the basics for personal hygiene, don't get me wrong – your showers (with scrubbing around the key areas), your deodorants, etc. – but I didn't take a huge amount of pride in my personal appearance.

I'm not sure why. Perhaps I had taken being fat to heart and there was no point in beautifying what I considered to be a bad canvas. Or, more likely, I was just a lazy young man. I also didn't take heroin, which is a shame because it would've at least helped keep my appetite down.

All that said, I don't think I was unhandsome. People insinuating that I was never held much water with me. Back when I was bigger, I still had the same face, there was just a hell of a lot more of it. Double handsome, if you ask me. If you saw me out and about these days wearing a big puffer coat and then saw me take it off, you wouldn't exclaim, 'Oh my God, you're actually really handsome!' Well, that's essentially what people did. I spent years wearing a big puffer coat made of myself. I've taken it off now, but it doesn't mean that I didn't love it when I was wearing it. I sure as hell miss it in the winter.

Those moments of shock from acquaintances were useful in some sense. They confirmed that what I was doing was working. When you are losing weight, it's very difficult to see any changes. I was weighing myself, yes. I think this was hugely unhelpful though. I would only really use the scales as a stick to beat myself with when I hadn't lost much or had even put on weight. Weighing ourselves is such an odd human habit. Literally calculating our mass as if we are checking the health of a new baby gorilla at the zoo. I would also use every single possible hack to cheat those scales. The worst habit I got into was making sure (and I'm sorry for the graphic nature of this) I had gone for a full and proper toilet before weighing myself. Some weeks when I had lost weight, I swear all I was doing was calculating the amount of toilet I had just done. I may as well have just squatted over the scales. An interesting experiment in its own right, but not what I was aiming for.

I don't weigh myself now. Down that road misery lies. It's been said by better and more eloquent people than I, but you do start to tie up your self-worth in those numbers. I'd sometimes have weeks where I'd not lost anything, or put on weight, and then write off those weeks as 'bad' ones. Whole batches of seven days consigned to the bin because an electronic appliance showed something on its digital display. Regardless of what else I'd done that particular week, I'd decide it was a bad one. That's no way to live. We still have scales in our house, but they're mainly used to weigh suitcases before we fly or to see how fat the cat is. Fat-shaming cats is funny and cool, and you can't convince me otherwise.

When it came to how I looked, I had no measure of how it was going other than those reactions from people I hadn't seen in a while. When you're that close to something, it's difficult to see incremental changes, let alone massive changes. They sneak up on you. Likewise with my girlfriend (now wife). Charlie saw me every day – there was no reason for her to wake up one morning and scream 'OH MY GOD!' as if it was some 1980s body-swap movie. There were a couple of clues now and again. It was only when I was losing weight that I realized I had bones in my wrists. For the first twenty-three years of my life they had been covered by a layer of lovely chub. When I hit a certain point in the process, some little bones started to poke through. My face revealed a jawline that I did not know existed. This is one of my features that I am sure I owe to the amount I used to eat. Two decades of chewing all day and night had clearly trained it up to mammoth size and all I had to do was reveal it to the world. To some extent, I think being bigger for so long was a real benefit. It's like I was encased in a protective layer. I emerged from my chrysalis looking much younger than my age, simply because I had been hidden from the world by my own body. I have started to look my age now, of course. Perhaps it's time to put the puffer jacket back on.

For the most part, though, it was more casual acquaintances who I relied upon to express their shock. Now, I've already said that I don't think asking people about their bodies is a good idea. I stand by that. However, it would be disingenuous of me to say that it didn't feel nice when people were complimentary or surprised. Because of course it did. Even when people asked if I was ill, there was a very dark part of my soul that enjoyed it. Maybe they mean I look ill, like one of the cool indie singers? It's an awful thing to admit, but when someone showed concern over my weight, I took some positives from it. Surely, I thought, that must mean I was smashing it? Am I so good at dropping the pounds that people are gravely concerned? Some of them simply didn't recognize me. I once had a full conversation with the comedian Mike Wozniak on Hungerford Bridge where he looked at me quizzically throughout. This isn't hugely unusual for a conversation with Mike, so I thought nothing of it. It was only when he texted me much later that I realized he had no clue who I was and was just being polite. Hours after our encounter something in his brain had twigged that it was me. He was mortified. He needn't have been though, because a couple of years later the same thing happened to me with him after he shaved off his moustache.

After I had lost the weight, my pride in my appearance definitely increased. I welcomed vanity into my life. This is definitely a potential downside. For my whole life I had been happy to do the bare minimum with the way I dressed and held myself. Those were easy times. I wore the same checked shirt and tatty jeans every day, and never felt any need to brush my hair. I scoffed at people spending money on clothes and using beauty products. To me, they were part of the pathetic mainstream and I was an edgy outsider who concerned himself with the things that really mattered. I didn't play their capitalist, image-obsessed game. As soon as I started to get compliments on how I looked, I dropped this outlook like a hot rock. As my weight decreased, my ego puffed up like a portobello mushroom in a bed of humid horseshit.

It's amazing, and depressing, how the way other people perceive you can change your own personality, but I'm afraid I fell into that trap. For the first time in my life I could walk into almost any shop and fit into clothes. This was genuinely exciting for a while. I shopped in all the places I used to make fun of people for going to. Before, I would be vicious about people who shopped in River Island

and Topman. They were cookie-cutter basic bitches with no thoughts of their own. They were swimming around in a murky pool of mediocrity, while I looked on smugly from my sun lounger, wearing tatty denim and an XXL Slipknot tee. The next thing I knew, I had stripped off my band merch and dived headlong into the pool with them. Bootcut was out, skinny jeans were in. I was walking into shops and browsing the clothes labelled M. To go from XL to M was quite the feeling. I'd skipped L! I was an M. M for medium, M for man, M for My God I've spent all my money on clothes again. It was a wondrous time. (These days I am in an L. L for Large, L for Legend, L for Let it go and have a burger once in a while.)

The sense of freedom was great, but at a certain point it faded. When you start focusing on your personal appearance, even in a positive way as I was, it leaves you open to doubt. You start to nit-pick. Before, I was happy with the way I looked because I had put no effort in. When I engaged in it, though, I started to worry that I hadn't done enough, or that I was wearing the wrong thing. Worse still, I started to worry that I was going to put on weight again. This is perhaps the most pointless thing you can put your brain through, but I didn't realize it at the time. I had worked hard to get to a certain point, but my brain was no longer letting me be proud of myself and enjoy it. It was telling me that I was going to go back to where I'd started. I wasn't doing anything differently, but I started to fear the idea of putting on weight again.

I distinctly remember the first time this happened. I was

doing a photoshoot for a show I was performing at the Edinburgh Festival. Photoshoots are an odd thing to go through as a comedian. Comedy is a profession that prides itself on not being about personal appearance – if you're funny, that's all that matters. Then suddenly you find yourself in a professional photography studio with big lights and a make-up artist and you realize that, sometimes, that is bullshit. Comedy at a certain level is obsessed with how people look. It's a public-facing industry and the public are obsessed with how people look. It stands to reason that appearance is going to be a factor in success, regardless of how little we like to admit it.

With all of this flying around my head, I found myself, for the first time in my life, spiralling about how I looked. I noticed a bit of my tummy poking out of the bottom of my T-shirt and that was enough. I was getting fat again, I decided. I looked no different to how I'd looked the previous day, when I was happy with my appearance. My brain had just played a trick on me. But at the time I didn't have the tools to deal with it like I do now. I thought my brain only told me things that were true. 'I am my brain and my brain is me,' I naively assumed. This isn't true. Sometimes, our brains are evil monsters that have risen up from a primordial bog determined to destroy us. They need to be reasoned with and compromised with until they sink back down into the gloop and leave us alone. I wasn't seeing any great change in my shape, all I was seeing was a bit of my body that I hadn't seen in that way before. It wasn't good or bad, it was just there. I also think that a T-shirt riding up and exposing a bit of skin is one of the most embarrassing things that can happen to a person, regardless of what their body type is. I feel ashamed when it happens to someone else. Embarrassed for them and ashamed of myself. *That is their secret skin! I deserve to go to prison and they need to buy a longer T-shirt.* These days I'm much better at dealing with these feelings when they arise. Bodies change all the time, that's just a fact.

FAT MAN BRAIN

My attitude to my appearance may have changed, but some things were destined to remain the same. It's true that I had to change my diet for ever to lose the weight and keep it off. I stopped bingeing and thought more consciously about what I was putting into my body. That sounds terribly wanky, but it's a fact. What could never change was my love of food. If anything, it massively increased.

The way I used to enjoy food was to gorge mindlessly on delicious junk. There is a huge amount of joy in this. To fully let go and tuck into piles of the sort of stuff we are told to avoid completely. To eat 'unhealthy' food with abandon is a middle finger to your parents and to the government. It's punk eating, and I was the Johnny Rotten of dinners. I loved food when I was fat. So, of course, when I lost weight it did not mean that that changed. Far from it. It's not something you can turn off like a tap. I was thinking about food all the time.

When I lost weight, though, I started to indulge in food in a new way. I started to appreciate good food, rather than lots of food. If I was going to have a burger in the past, I would eat the most convenient burger, and then probably another one (and, let's be honest, another one). When I changed my diet, I would do my research and eat the best burger I could find. Food became a genuine hobby and interest. I would read articles, ask for recommendations, explore restaurants. Yes, I became a food wanker. My love of good food increased exponentially, and I could barely talk about anything else. When you're not eating everything all of the time you learn to value those moments of indulgence. I wasn't going to waste those glorious treat meals on something substandard, I was going to find the most delicious and well-made food I could lay my hands on. To me, this makes sense. My life's goal was now to fully immerse myself in good food. It was as if I had become that seven-year-old salmon-eating gourmand again. To my friends and family, I'd imagine, I turned into a total bore. However, same friends and family will still text me for restaurant recommendations. Hypocrites.

The bingeing inclination is never far from the surface though. Because even though I changed physically, I still have a fat-man brain. That will never be altered. For the first twenty-three years of my life I ate anything and everything that was put in front of me. I would never leave a single morsel, regardless of how full I was. I don't know the psychological reason for this. As I've mentioned, it almost felt like it was driven by a fear that I would never get to eat that thing again. That makes sense if you are eating in a place you might not get to visit again – a fancy restaurant, or when you're on holiday. Such experiences are finite. There is a chance that if you're abroad and you have managed to find an amazing dish, you will never get to have it again. You should eat all of it and then order another. But this was not the only time I did this. I would do it with a big bag of crisps from the local shop. I could have nipped round the corner and got another bag at any time, so why was I so determined to finish them?

My dad is the same, so maybe I can blame him? His excuse is that he was a child in the 1950s at the tail end of rationing, so he can never leave an empty plate for fear of not getting anything else, and for the guilt of being wasteful. It was drummed into him at an early age, he says, so now he must absolutely decimate every meal he is presented with. This seems like a very convenient excuse, but it hangs together nonetheless. It's not something I can claim for myself. I was a child of the 1990s, a time of absolutely no hardship for me. I was brought up in a privileged household where I always knew where my next meal was coming from, in a time of relative calm globally. What can I say? That I have to eat a lot because when I was a child I wanted to be as big as Shadow from *Gladiators*? Maybe that I have to clean my plate because of something Trevor and Simon said on *Live & Kicking*? There's no explanation for it. I was just greedy.

I still am greedy. I've managed to curb some of my impulses, but that is who I am as a person. My body may be different, but I always feel uncomfortable in the company of the thin. Thinness, as far as I can see it, has nothing to do with how you actually look. It is a state of mind. A state of mind that I do not have. Thinness is being at a party and not spending all night by the snacks. Thinness is sharing dishes at restaurants with other thinnies. Thinness is vodka soda. If this is indeed the checklist, I am not thin at my core. I am still fat. Among such people I feel like I have been sent as an undercover operative by the larger community to infiltrate the slender underground to gather information on them. I'm not great at being undercover though. It's a surprise to me that I haven't been ushered into the office of the thin boss and been taken out. I'm always the guy ordering too much in restaurants, always the guy finishing everyone else's meals. These are simply impulses I will never lose, and nor would I want to.

Now and again I really get to flex my fat-man credentials. In 2022 I was hired as a permanent judge on *Great British Menu*, one of the jewels in the BBC's television food output. The job involves being presented with dish after dish cooked by some of the best chefs in the UK. A typical day consists of eight to ten plates, from 10 a.m. to 5 p.m. I was warned on day one to eat only a few bites of each, lest I become too full by the end of the day to be able to judge effectively. They clearly didn't know who they were dealing with. In my first series as a judge I demolished everything. I couldn't help myself. I tried to tell everyone that I was a child of the 1990s, but they just looked at me quizzically. Even when I was not fully enjoying one of the courses, I couldn't stop myself finishing it. Not only finishing it but also drinking the sauce and licking the plate. By the time the next series came around, I convinced myself that I would be more frugal and refined. I would take a few dainty bites, consider the flavours, make some erudite comments on technique and then put down the knife and fork. The novelty had worn off, I told myself. I think you see where this is going. Come day one of my second series, I nailed everything.

It's like I have something within my chemical make-up that makes me finish every bit of food in front of me. And you know what? I don't think this is a bad thing. As long as I am enjoying food, I am enjoying life. I'd much rather be this person than someone for whom food is a chore and something from which they take no real pleasure. For all my struggles with weight in the past, I wouldn't trade the elation food brings me for anything. In order to maintain this passion at this level, though, I had to force myself to enjoy something else.

6

JUDO PORK SHOULDER

I'm ashamed to say it, but I enjoy exercise. This feels like the worst thing I could possibly admit. I used to be vehemently anti-exercise and anti all the people who did it regularly. To me, they were wasting their lives. As far as I could see it, every time I had done exercise it felt horrible. Why would I do something that made me feel horrible? It seemed counter-intuitive. In every other area, we are told that feeling bad is to be avoided at all costs. So why would these people deliberately punish themselves on the reg? They clearly had something seriously wrong in their psyches. And they always seemed so smug when they did it! Why would I want to be one of those snooty, panting little kiss-arses? They certainly seemed mighty proud of themselves for someone who was bright red and covered in sweat. If I was going to get out of breath, I was going to do it the correct way. Running to the door to collect my takeaway.

I think part of it must be how exercise is enforced on us at a young age. At school, it was never presented as something fun to do (certainly not at my school). It was something we *had* to do. It was never taught to us that we could explore what we enjoyed and pursue that, it was just another subject. This inevitably meant we were immediately ranked by ability. This feels very unfair and sucks any potential enjoyment out of it from the get-go. I was terrible at maths and realized early on that I was always going to be near the bottom of the class. This had the knock-on effect that I was just never going to try. Exactly the same thing happened with sports. I was not naturally gifted, something that was exacerbated by my weight. So, I gave up. Even in sports where size is occasionally venerated, like rugby, I did not excel. Once this was spotted, I was put in a lower team and left to fester. By the time I left school, I hated sport, and as a result hated all physical activity. By the time I got to university, nobody was making me do any, so my weight increased and with it my disinclination to do any exercise whatsoever. It's a vicious circle, and a vicious circle is what I became.

They made me do cross-country, for God's sake! Every week, they bundled us all on to the common and forced us to run for miles. When you're much younger, running is fun. You run around with your friends playing tag or booting a football in the playground. This is good because the running is a by-product of spending time with your friends. There is no coercion and no formalizing of what should be a laugh. Cross-country was evil. My main issue with it as a school activity was that there was no actual *teaching* involved. At least in every other subject the teachers made some effort to improve your abilities. With cross-country, there was none of that. The rangy, skinny kids who were naturally more effective runners would win every week, leaving me and the rest of the fat kids languishing at the rear feeling terrible about ourselves. Nobody ever took us to one side to hone our running techniques or buy us better trainers. We were just the worst week after week. That sort of thing gets to you. On the upside, it really allowed me to work on my smoking. My friend Josh and I would deliberately go slowly, until we were out of sight at the back of the field, and light up. We could get through three or four Marlboro Lights before the end of the course. This obviously had further negative effects on our running abilities, but we didn't care.

I don't see why we have to abandon playground games. As soon as you enforce exercise and start ranking kids, the enjoyment is obviously going to be destroyed for those less naturally blessed. Far be it from me to revolutionize the entire education system, but here goes. Those playground games we play when we're younger should be the sole sports offered at school. There would be no official competition, no teams, just an hour a day where everyone runs around and has fun. They would still get the benefit of the exercise without any of the crushing realization at a formative age that they are bad at something. If you absolutely have to introduce competitive team sports, at least throw in a couple for the less physically gifted. Dodgeball? Hide-and-seek? A competitive-eating team perhaps? I know that my self-esteem would've been much less fragile after school if I had come out with a medal for the most hot dogs eaten at the National Schools Pig Out 1999. And if my school had offered a team-based smoking trophy? Forget about it. My name would now be on a plaque outside the science labs. 'This school was attended by Ed Gamble, who holds the school record for most cigs chained in half an hour.'

I did try exercise briefly at university. I was buoyed by the opportunity to create a new personality for myself, and the freedom of choosing a sport from the huge range of options available. I settled on judo. My dad had done it in the past and I liked the idea of my size being an advantage. I duly waddled off to an introductory session during Freshers' Week, determined that this was the start of a new me.

When I arrived, there was an immediate problem. Every-one else had clearly done judo in the past and had brought their own judogi (fun judo costume). I didn't have one, obviously. I was led to believe that this was a session for beginners and had gone on a whim. They assured me that this wasn't a problem and went into the back of the studio to dig me out some lost property. This didn't fill me with hope. All I could think was why someone would lose their judo kit? Either they had left it there, never to return (not a great sign for my new hobby), or they had died during a class. Things got worse when it became evident that they had nothing that would fit me. In front of the rest of the increasingly impatient class I tried on a series of tiny outfits, all of which made me look like a tightly wrapped pork shoulder. We eventually decided that for this session I would wear what I'd arrived in (a Cradle of Filth hoodie) and then go away and buy my own uniform, presumably from a specialist website for hippos who want to do martial arts. Then, when I came back for the next class, I could wear that. I happily agreed, already knowing at this point that there was no way I was coming back and looking these people in the eye ever again.

They then paired us off to spar, without telling me any of the basics of judo. The boy I was put with had been doing judo for five years, had won championships and was clearly very satisfied with this. He was, however, significantly smaller than me. I cannot tell you the glee that filled my soul for the next hour while he tried every single move in his repertoire on me, to absolutely no avail. It was a textbook example of why there are weight classes in combat sports. I simply stood there, doing nothing, while he scuttled up and down my ample frame, desperately trying to knock me to the ground. Every so often I would deliberately fall over for a little rest, but I made sure to do it at a moment when he was in no doubt that it was because of nothing he had done. He may as well have been doing judo on a wall.

I enjoyed this, but I knew in my heart that I couldn't show my face there again. In fact, that was the end of my university sporting career. I instead fell headlong into writing and performing sketch comedy, which definitely set me on the career path that led me to where I am now. Famously, though, it's not great cardio.

My exercise journey only began in earnest around the time I started to try and lose weight. Remarkably, against all odds, I stuck at it. I felt mildly ashamed. After years of sneering at people who exercise, here I was. I joined a gym and I started walking. To be honest, I was mainly walking to the gym and walking on the treadmill and then walking home. It was a lot of walking. It would've been cheaper not to join a gym and just walk past it every day, but I liked the idea of being in a gym. It was alien territory to me. Yet again, I felt like an undercover agent. I would still sneer at the other people there – the weights people, the exercise-bike people, the Zumba people. All of them were recipients of dirty looks from my ivory tower (a treadmill set to 1.5 kilometres per hour). I think we're beginning to see a pattern here. Just like the healthy eaters, I was mocking them, completely unaware that I was destined to become one of them.

I started small with exercise. I was terrified of overdoing it and keeling over. I had noticed significant changes by making alterations to my diet, and I was still eating what many people would consider a lot of food. It wasn't a drastic change in lifestyle, and I was sure that the same would go for exercise. Even a little bit from a standing start was going to help. I was proved right.

I got the idea from an interview I'd seen with darts legend Andy Fordham (aka The Viking). Fordham was an absolute mountain of a man and had made the decision to try to improve his health. In the interview (as I remember it), he said that his personal trainer had started by making him get in and out of a chair a few times a day. This, of course, sounded ridiculous – the idea that someone's first step of a workout was simply getting out of a chair. But the more I thought about it, the more inspirational I found it. Firstly, that Andy Fordham would even admit this publicly when he must've known that it sounded a bit silly. That took bravery. But it made sense! He was a big guy who was clearly doing very little other than walking back and forth between a dartboard and the oche. Any physical activity, however small, was going to make a difference. My second thought was that his personal trainer was not qualified and was taking the piss. He'd panicked, looked around the room and spotted a chair. 'That'll do,' he'd thought. Either way, this interview oddly inspired me just to start doing *something* and building it from there. I won't enjoy it, I told myself, but I'll do it.

I'll never be the sort of guy who enjoys exercise, I'll stick to walking, I thought. It seemed to be working and it was a nice opportunity to listen to music and collect my thoughts. I'll never run. Why will I run? You know who runs? Dickheads. People on Facebook who ask you to sponsor them. Men having a breakdown in Lycra. That's not me, I thought.

Then one morning, on the way to the gym, I remembered that I wasn't allowed to go that day. This wasn't as religious as it sounds. I had signed up for one of those off-peak memberships, which allowed you to attend the gym only on weekdays between nine and five. Essentially, when most people are at work doing their actual jobs. I was making my first tentative steps towards being a professional comedian, so this was ideal. That is one of the major benefits of being a comedian: you get access to spaces in the day that are, by and large, free of most other people. If you were to ask me why I became a comedian, I would say, 'I loved comedy and wanted to make people laugh.' Ask me why I still want to be a comedian now, however, and the answer will always be the same: 'Empty cinema.' The off-peak membership was crucial to me starting to exercise. What always worried me about working out was other people seeing. That's the reason I hated it at school, and the reason I never returned to judo. Even to this day I find it almost impossible to do any physical activity with other eyes on me. So, to be able to go to the gym when the only people in there were me and the occasional old man was ideal. I don't mind old people seeing the horror of me on a treadmill. They've seen so much. Once you'd experienced the Blitz, the sight of a fat man assaulting a running machine would seem like nothing.

On this occasion, though, I had got my days mixed up and had started to head off to the gym on a Saturday. I couldn't go in, but I was still determined to do something. An odd side-effect of starting this new lifestyle was an increased willpower which I had no idea was within me. I had always given up on stuff halfway through, or consciously phoned it in for fear of failing. Now, though, I was pushing myself. I was keeping what I was doing very quiet, which was key. If nobody knew I was trying to lose weight, it would not matter if it didn't work out. I couldn't imagine

the embarrassment of constantly posting about my 'journey' on social media, as so many people do. I understand
the logic behind it – they are holding themselves to account
by telling other people. But this is using the fear of other
people seeing them fail to drive them, which I didn't fancy.
I much preferred the quiet method of losing weight by
stealth. People would find out if I'd been successful, and
then they could ask me if I was ill. This clandestine mission
I had given myself was the right way of going about it. I
was totally responsible for what I was doing, and if it didn't
work out, that was fine. Nobody would tell me off. Because
of this, I found it much easier to maintain the regime.

So, on this day, even though the gym was out of bounds
to me, I still decided something was better than nothing. I
went to the park, and before I knew it, I was running. I say
'running'. To all intents and purposes it was fast walking,
or a turbo waddle. In my head, I was an elegant gazelle.
Having seen pictures of myself running since, this is not
accurate. If a gazelle ever saw me running it would be massively offended. This was not the sort of run that would
help me escape a lion. I would be chunks of meat within
seconds. All hope of escaping the lion would rest on it finding my ridiculous jog so hilarious that it lost its mind
laughing and had to steady itself with two paws on a rock.
Only then would I make my exit to safety.

For the first five minutes of the turbo waddle, I hated it.
Everything I had thought about running and runners was
confirmed to me in those moments. It was, as I had
expected, self-harm for psychopaths. I was out of breath,

my chest was burning, and I couldn't see for sweat. Who would do this? Then, something happened. I found a rhythm, albeit a painfully slow one. I started to listen to the music in my headphones and enjoy the view across the Thames. The adverse physical effects I was feeling started to become positives in my mind. I was exercising! I was really doing it! Was this the runner's high that everyone talked about? It felt like a mixture of adrenalin and smug superiority – this must be it! I was flying. Against every moral fibre of my being and personality, I was a runner! Then, I shit my pants.

I need you to know that I am not speaking metaphorically. I actually shit my pants. It's not that I got a fright and have now decided to use the figurative phrase 'I shit my pants'. I did get a fright, but it was as a direct result of literally shitting my pants. It happened with absolutely no warning flare. Normally, if you have a dicky tummy or an emergency toilet situation, there is a whisper from your body that it might happen. A rumour starts to spread around your lower intestines that you might be in trouble. Usually by way of a familiar gurgle, so you have time to get to an appropriate location. On this occasion, my body let me down completely. There was no announcement, it skipped straight to the event. To say I was shocked is an understatement. Many thoughts ran through my head. This was the first time I had been for a run – does this happen every time? Is this what runners have to put up with? I had started to enjoy myself, sure, but now I wasn't convinced it was worth it. What a trade-off that would be, if every time you embarked on a run you were a hundred per cent certain you were going to soil yourself. Maybe, I thought, that's why runners always look so pained. They are either in a state, or they know they are about to shit themselves, or they have just shit themselves. But surely this couldn't be the case? I thought of all those elite marathon runners I'd seen on TV. They were grimacing, of course, but I was sure that was just the exertion. They were wearing those tiny little shorts, too. Absolutely nobody who was certain that they were going to poop themselves would put on minuscule shorts that ride all the way up their thigh. If shitting was a dead cert while you were running, everyone would surely start the marathon wearing MC Hammer trousers tied off at the ankle. Maybe this only happened the first time people went for a run? My body wasn't used to this level of exertion at all. It must have assumed that if I was running, then I was in trouble. It must have initiated a protocol that has resided with humans since caveman times. For all my body knew, I was dashing away from a predator, so it decided to offload any extra weight to help me in my escape. This would also have the benefit of leaving a noxious obstacle in my wake, designed to put off whatever was chasing me. A bit like a banana skin in Mario Kart.

Whatever was happening to me, I needed to sort it out as soon as possible. My first thought was to gingerly climb down into the Thames and wade about until I was clean. Those of you who have seen the Thames know that this would've been a pointless thing to do. I may have been able to leave my faeces behind, but I'd've come out with a lot more than I went in with (a shopping trolley, Weil's disease, evidence in a murder). It was too far for me to get home without some sort of spillage incident.

Then, I was hit by a stroke of genius. It's very difficult to claim any level of genius as an adult man who has shat his pants, granted. Even if a scientist came up with a cure for cancer tomorrow, I'm not sure it would even make it to clinical trials if it turned out he had poo in his trousers. Even for a clean-panted man, my idea probably couldn't be considered genius, even though I thought it was at the time. I remembered that this park had a public toilet. Surely I could clean myself up in there? It wasn't too far away – I could make it look like I was injured and limp slowly towards it. There weren't many other people around, but even if they saw me, they would just assume I had run too hard and pulled a muscle (as long as they didn't get within sniffing distance).

Thanks to my natural affinity for acting and espionage, I made it to the toilet without being rumbled. Even more fortuitously, it was empty. I locked the main door and looked round, still unsure of what to do. I had inadvertently created the worst escape room of all time. For those of you who don't know, public conveniences in parks are not pleasant places. Most public toilets aren't exactly dreamy, but the ones in parks are the lowest of the low. Counter-intuitively, that's because people rarely actually go to the toilet in them. Park public toilets are usually frequented by people who want to take drugs, have illicit sexual encounters or just simply chuck a load of stuff about and smash a mirror. This place was no exception. What I was about to do was bleak, and the surroundings matched it.

Logic dictated that I go into a cubicle, clean myself up as much as possible with toilet paper, cut my losses and head home as quickly as possible. I was lucky enough to be alone, so I needed to act quickly before a passer-by arrived. Unfortunately, this is where my luck ran out. No paper. No. Paper. The one thing that was essential to my plan of cleaning up my pants and going home to forget this ever happened. I was in exactly the same situation as before I'd had my stroke of genius.

There was only one thing for it. I'm not proud of this. I'll just tell you quickly so it's over with: I took off my underpants and left them in the cistern of the toilet. I always knew I would be a bad murderer, but this confirmed it. I was panicking and immediately hid the evidence near the scene of the crime. If that was a hammer, I'd be down for a ten stretch. Somehow, in this disgusting public bog, I had provided it with its most disgusting feature. I did everything I could to conceal what I had done, put my tracksuit trousers back on and ran home the fastest I had ever run, not stopping to think about what I would do if this sprinting initiated a second wave. Thinking about it now, I probably should've put my trousers on *before* I started to rearrange the cistern. Being caught putting shitty clothes in a toilet would've been bad enough, but imagine if someone had walked in to find a man doing that while naked from the waist down like Winnie the Pooh. (There's a joke there that even I won't degrade you with.)

I never returned to that toilet. The next few nights after the incident were restless and nightmare-filled. I would imagine innocent people going into the toilet, discovering my shame pants and being scarred for life. I considered sneaking back under the cover of darkness and removing the offending article, but I could never quite bring myself to do it. Returning to the scene of the crime is how most criminals are caught, I decided, and it was just too risky a course of action. I also momentarily considered burning the toilet down, so nobody would ever have to encounter my misdeed. Again, now I think about it, this is probably the reason for most deliberate fires. They will never admit it, but people who burn buildings down are trying to destroy evidence of their incontinence. Arson should be renamed arsen.

You would've thought that all this would have put me off running for life, but it didn't. After some extensive googling about people who had similar issues, I discovered a complicated and little-known technique to stop it happening the next time I went for a run. Go to the toilet *before* the run. Crazy, right? I started running a few times a week. As I did so, I began to break through that horrible bit at the start quicker and quicker. I was actually enjoying it. I felt like I was betraying some past version of myself. I was feeling this a lot at that time. My decision to lose weight was accompanied by a feeling of guilt that I was letting down the man who was actually quite positive about being bigger, as well as abandoning my friends who were a simi-lar size. They were (mainly) supportive of what I was doing, but there was a sense within me that I was breaking some sort of unspoken code that fatties stick together. We would laugh at thin people who exercised and who were wasting their lives and punishing themselves by not eating whatever they wanted. Then, in my mind, I turned my back on my crew. I switched allegiance to the dark side. I con-soled myself with the fact that while I may be running now and again, I wasn't a *runner.* That is a very different type of person. I just happened to be running. I wasn't one of those runners who has special trainers and does marathons. At least I still had the marathon people to sneer at. I would never be one of them.

The first time I ran the London Marathon was in 2017. The ultimate betrayal of myself. Not a lot of people enter a marathon while bandying around words like 'betrayal' or 'scab', but that's how I felt. It's a pattern I find myself fol-lowing repeatedly in my life. I make fun of people for doing something then a couple of years later I end up doing it with a great sense of shame (losing weight, marathons, getting married, vaping). I suppose you can see this as a warning. If you snigger behind people's backs, it may pre-vent you from adopting their positive behaviours in the future. You'll fear you will look like a turncoat. Worst of all, if you make fun of people for doing something, you will ultimately live with the fear that other people are doing that to you further down the line. This advice doesn't apply to vaping, by the way. I shouldn't do that. It looks ridiculous and offers me no benefits whatsoever. Please make fun of me behind my back for doing that, I deserve it. I guess my very specific advice there would be don't go on *Live at the Apollo* and deliver a routine that eviscerates people for vaping, only to take it up yourself a few years later. You'll look like a total idiot.

Fear of being seen as the sort of person I used to make fun of nearly prevented me from doing the marathon. The fact that I had agreed to do it for charity is what convinced me – I didn't want to let them down. Plus, the charity in question was JDRF UK, a type 1 diabetes charity. As a type 1 diabetic, something we'll get into later, I knew I would get the money back eventually.

I followed my training plan to the letter. As much as I harp on about being a comedian and the freedom and agency that career allows, I am *very* good at following the rules. Rules make me feel safe. As long as I'm following the rules, I feel like every day I am getting the little pat on the back that I constantly crave. I often think I would've been better off joining the military. I would have loved a daily set of commands to follow, the outfits are nice, and they make their beds every morning with real panache. The potentially having to kill someone puts me off a bit, but maybe I could've told them that and been recruited exclusively to the bed-making regiment. I didn't join the military of course, and in reality I don't think I would've got on that well. I have what my wife has described as 'the flattest feet she has ever seen'. I never knew this was an issue until one day when she spotted my wet footprints after I'd got out of a swimming pool. Apparently, most people's footprints are just the toes, the heel and the edge of the arch that links them. Mine were an entire, full foot. According to her, I have the feet of a duck.

Despite having webbed flippers, a broken pancreas and the bowels of a baby, I persevered with training for the marathon. As much as I loved the training, the actual day did not go exactly as planned. My bowels didn't act up, thank God. I had long mastered the art of keeping clean pants (aged thirty-one), which was lucky as it would've been difficult to dispose of dirty knickers among a hundred thousand other people. Even the flat feet didn't seem to bother me, despite later seeing official event photos which made it very clear that I run like a big goose. The problems came at around mile five. I was waddling along very nicely indeed and soaking up the unbelievable atmosphere. Being diabetic definitely makes the marathon a trickier experience, however. Physical activity can reduce your blood glucose, so running for so long puts you in danger of it reaching a harmful level. If this had happened, it would've ended the day early for me. Luckily I had trained for this, so was constantly testing my blood around the course and topping up on sugary energy drinks as needed. It was a difficult balance, because if my blood glucose were to go too high, that would have made me sluggish and unable to perform in the way that I wanted.

I'd love to be able to tell you that the issues were due to my medical condition. At least that would get me some sympathy. Sadly, the reality is far more slapstick than that.

I had grabbed a bottle of water and a bottle of Lucozade Sport from one of the many drink stations along the route. One in each hand, I was constantly refreshing myself with the water and topping up my sugar with the Lucozade. At some point I got the idea that I would like to douse myself in water. It would cool me down and have the added bonus of looking extremely sexy. I'm sure you see where this is going. Swept away by the adrenalin of the day, I got confused and soaked myself in Lucozade. The next twenty-one miles were among the stickiest I have ever experienced. While it wasn't the height of summer, it was an unseasonably hot day, making this even more unpleasant. One bee chased me for what felt like ten miles. I think it was the first I had seen that year, and the last one until about July. So potent was the sweet stink of my skin, this bee had been roused from whatever hibernation bees are in during the colder months.

I should stress, this was an actual bee and not someone dressed as a bee. There were plenty of people wearing novelty costumes that day, but as far as I'm aware there was no one dressed like a bee who was so deep in character that they decided to pursue me. Being overtaken by runners dressed in ridiculous outfits is a rite of passage in the London Marathon and my experience was no different. I was beaten by a chef carrying a pan, a lady dressed as a turtle, and a giant padlock (gender unconfirmed). By mile twenty-three I myself had taken on a costume. I was disguised as a man who regretted every single life choice that had led him to this point. I was a physical wreck, not to mention stickier and sweeter than a post-dip Augustus Gloop.

It was at this point that the leg cramp kicked in. I had never felt pain like it. My left leg seized up completely, shooting lightning bolts of agony down my thigh and right into the bottom of my duck feet. How I managed to continue is, to this day, beyond me. I had to stop and stretch, which did not work. Starting running again after that was one of the hardest physical things I've ever had to do. My body was screaming at me to stop. Of course it was. Only a few years earlier it had been used to doing nothing all day apart from welcoming paninis on an hourly basis, and now it was being forced to run an inhuman number of miles. This is not what my body had signed up for. I had to run the last three miles with one straight leg, like I was doing some sort of bizarre mating-ritual dance. I finished. I may have betrayed my former self, but I take comfort from the fact that I did it in the most demeaning and degrading way possible. It was an achievement, but it was an achievement Gamble style.

Afterwards, I ate like I was a teenager again. This, for me, is the true meaning of and reason for exercise. So many people use it as a way of keeping their weight down and run it concurrently with a restrictive diet. While I did this initially, it did not last long. I need joy in my life. I get some joy from exercise, but absolutely nothing rivals the absolute elation I feel when I eat something delicious. Working out, for me, adds a shine to that elation. It makes me hungrier, meaning I can consume a lot more of the delicious things. Why would you want to live your life with just the exercise? There's nothing I love more than riding the high from working out by adding the sparkling bliss of a delicious meal. I'm not advocating only eating well if you've exercised, by the way. Food as a reward for exercise is a dangerous path. But exercising and then denying yourself the pleasures of food is very odd behaviour.

I will never be the kind of person who places a love of exercise ahead of my love of food. However guilty I feel about enjoying working out now, I still have a robust disdain for the truly healthy. I am, and shall remain, utterly food-focused. And when I say 'focused', that's somewhat of an understatement. It would be like referring to Gollum as 'ring curious' or to Fred West as a 'patio enthusiast'.

I'm taking it on trust that if you are reading this book, then you share my passion for food, which means we can safely discuss those 'other' people. You know who I mean. Quickly check around you and make sure that none of them are reading over your shoulder. They're easy to spot – they'll be wearing gym clothes like normal clothes. We clear? OK, let's slag them off.

You know the type I'm talking about. I call them 'The Fuellers'. This is a nickname based on their favourite phrase – 'Food is just fuel.' This is normally an immediate alarm bell for me in a conversation. If I am chatting to someone and hear this, it's a DEFCON 1 situation. I drop whatever I'm holding, scream and point to distract their attention away from me, then make for the door, or if needs be, crash through a plate-glass window.

'Food is just fuel.' Repeat that out loud a few times; really let it roll around your mouth. It never gets any less weird, does it? These are people who don't really like food. I simply don't understand it. If you don't like food, then what do you think about all of the time? My entire day is structured around what I'm eating and when I eat it. The moment I wake up, my thoughts turn to breakfast. I consult my mental Rolodex of what I have in and begin compiling potential dishes. (By 'mental Rolodex', I mean an imagined Rolodex, not a real Rolodex – that is also bonkers. A real Rolodex which details all of your groceries would be mental, despite it being an idea that I now want to follow up on.) Frankly, most mornings, the thought of the first meal of the day is what gets me out of bed. What is motivating the Fuellers? It surely can't be breakfast. I can't imagine anyone bounding out from under their duvet electrified and giddy at the prospect of 'morning fuel'. For the first bite of breakfast, I'm in the moment, enjoying the food. By the second bite, I'm back to the bonkers Rolodex and dreaming up lunch. This will occupy my thoughts until I am eating it. Food is not only the structure to my day, it is the fabric and substance of it. For the Fuellers, food is an annoyance. They willingly admit that they only eat it because without it they would die. Not exactly the sort of person you'd want to invite out for a slap-up meal.

In my mind, most of life's great joys are based on food or centred around it. Christmas dinner with family, lunch with friends, long boozy meals on holiday – all are responsible for some of my most cherished memories. I certainly do not want to spend my time with anyone who is coming to meet me at a restaurant for a couple of hours of 'stopping themselves dying'.

This is not to say that Fuellers are not nice people. Take my friend Joel. He is a wonderful talent, a lovely man and someone I would count as a dear friend. He is also the most insanely ripped person in the world. Nobody outside the world of statues should look like Joel. Joel, as you may have guessed, is a Fueller. Everything he puts into his mouth is balanced perfectly to fit in with his daily plan, which is machine-tooled to make his muscles look all nice and handsome. I love spending time with Joel, I just know how and when to do it. For instance, I would never invite him to a restaurant I am excited about. Firstly, he won't appreciate it, and secondly, he will probably sneak off halfway through to eat a Tupperware full of steamed chicken breast in the toilet. No, Joel is not a restaurant friend. He likes being kind and lifting heavy things. Joel is a moving-house friend.

There is an instinct many of us have, especially in Britain, to mock the health conscious. We take it personally that they are not binge-eating and drinking, seeing it as an affront to our own more indulgent lifestyles. But we have to realize that these people need our help. Next time you see someone coming out of a Crossfit gym or drinking a protein shake, please resist the urge to taunt them. Be kind, remember what they are going through, and buy them some cheese.

Some Fuellers, however, don't reveal themselves as plainly as Joel. They've learnt not to use the 'fuel' phrase in public, lest they are made into a pariah. They have other, more subtle tells and catchphrases. Luckily, I am an expert at rooting out these slugs and can tell you what to listen out for. What follows is a short checklist, to let you know whether there is a Fueller in your life.

- *I would take food in pill form if I could.* This is something I've heard from a few people over the years. The suggestion being that food is such a bother to them, such an administrative nightmare, that they would rather pop a pill if it filled them up enough to sustain them. This is infuriating on a few levels. It's normally said by someone who is bragging about how busy they are on a day-to-day basis, which is a whole different category of egg. They are so busy, they claim, that the act of keeping themselves alive is too much hassle. They don't have time even to chew, let alone enjoy the taste of what they're eating. I find it bizarre that anybody is too busy to enjoy food or take a break to have a meal. It should be what you look forward to. For me, work and life get in the way of food. If admin clearance was available in pill form, I'd take it. I race through everything to get to meals quicker. In fact, I'm writing this chapter in haste, simply because I'm making a curry later and I can't wait. If I ever do take pills, it will be to prolong my life so I have more time to eat more food. I imagine that food will eventually kill me, I just plan on that happening in the distant future, and largely because of cheese. I want them to cut me open and have to call in medical students to marvel at the man who is somehow part fondue.

- *I think we have some biscuits, I'll just go and check.* This is normally deployed when you enter a Fueller's abode. Just like we can sense them, they can spot us a mile off. It's usually uttered in a withering tone, as if to suggest 'I don't normally eat snacks, I'm far too healthy, but I suppose I could be accommodating seeing as we have a biscuit person in our midst.' 'Why is this bad?' I hear you ask. 'They have biscuits. Surely anyone who has treats is not a misery-monger?' Look again at the statement. 'I think I have some biscuits, I'll just go and check.' They *think* they have some biscuits. If there is anyone reading this now who only *thinks* they have some biscuits in the house, put this book down. You should know exactly what food you have in every corner of your living space, especially when it comes to baked goods. I have a detailed and accurate mental blueprint of everything edible in my house, a sort of calorie-laden Sherlock mind palace. In an emergency, I could grab all of the important things. There's a fire? Biscuits, chocolate, cheese, ice cream and the chocolate I keep secret from my girlfriend are in the bag. Then, of course, the bacon (after the fire has sizzled it up a treat). Then I'll wake Charlie and let her know the situation. Another issue with this statement: who has biscuits long enough actually to put them away? The journey of the biscuit should be thus: factory to packet to shop to trolley to bag to car to mouth. Strictly, a cupboard should be involved only for back-up biscuits. And if even they stay there for more than a day or so, I consider you some sort of Mr Miyagi-level Zen master.

- *Can we get that dessert with two spoons?* Throw down your napkin and get out of the restaurant. The evening is over. Sharing food is a big issue for me, and one that I'll be delving into in more detail later in this book. There are some instances where sharing starters, main courses and sides is a delight. But if you want to have a dessert, you have a whole dessert to yourself. And no, you don't get to have a 'taste' of mine, like that suddenly doesn't count. You don't get to have all the pleasure of a taste of the dessert without taking on the bulk of the calories and accompanying guilt. You're playing with the big boys now, and big boys order their own pudding and take responsibility. There is one exception: the whole dessert menu order. Strap in, because this is some advanced stuff. I have only been part of a whole dessert menu order twice in my life, both times with James Acaster. We are the perfect combination for eating together in restaurants. We are both greedy, we love leading each other astray, and we are both incredibly weak-willed. The whole dessert menu order is exactly as it sounds: paralysed by the choice of sweet options, you order everything listed on the menu and then share it all. Everyone should do this at least once in their life. The feeling it gives you is magical. You have to do it right – please don't order everything individually. You have to say 'all of them', or 'one of each', and then toss the menu back on to the table like you do this every time. Then comes the hardest bit: concealing your absolute giddy glee at having done this until the waiter leaves. If you order the menu and then burst out laughing, or even smile at the person you're with, the magic is lost. Hold the server's gaze, while they marvel at what a maverick you are. As soon as they turn their back, though, high-five the hell out of each other, safe in the knowledge that for the next twenty-four hours you will feel like Jay-Z must feel every day of his life. Not exactly like Jay-Z though. My life is less popping bottles and more popping Rennies.

These sorts of people are best avoided. The irony being, when I started to lose weight and get healthy, everyone assumed I had become one of those people. They thought I had become a health bore. The fact is, all getting healthier did for me was focus my resolve to eat and drink the best of everything. My eating went from being a quantity-based hobby to being an absolute all-consuming obsession. A health bore I was not, but a food bore? Absolutely. Still terrible company on a night out, but at least I was tedious about something delicious. I was baguettes before biceps and I put the ham in hamstrings. I loved this new era of my life. There was one thing, though, that I was determined not to become obsessed with.

7

THE WINE LIST

Wine is a divisive topic. To some it is the pinnacle of respectable and discerning drinking, while to others it represents the height of pomposity and pretentious bullshit. The truth is, it's somewhere in between. That's always the let-down when it comes to divisive topics. We live in an increasingly binary age, but most things are 'somewhere in between'. However, it's way more fun to take sides and get angry than to sit on a fence, so let's do that instead.

I'll admit that when it comes to wine, I do indulge in the pretentious bullshit, while remaining self-aware that the whole enterprise is utterly ridiculous. I don't know exactly when I switched sides, as I used to be a fully signed up member of the anti-wine crew. I couldn't work out why anyone would choose wine over beer or Diet Coke, and the idea of someone smelling a wine and talking about it filled me with a distinct ick. This opinion was fortified (like a fine port) when I saw the fantastic documentary film *Somm*. I would recommend watching it to both sides of the wine binary. It follows sommeliers on their journey to their exams to become 'Masters of Wine' and you find yourself quite swept up in the fates of these objectively ridiculous characters. Despite my belief that what they were obsessed with was built on a house of sand, I still found the depth of their dedication quite admirable. The actual content of what they were doing, though, was insane.

In a moment that will live with me for ever more, one of the students pours himself a glass of white wine and declares that it smells like 'a freshly opened can of tennis balls'. Is there a more perfect encapsulation of why people hate wine bullshit? Wine's reputation is that it is for the rich and privileged, and by comparing its aroma to an equally privileged reference point this chap had totally put the final nail in the wine coffin for me. He may as well have said it was a little like 'freshly killed fox on the nose', or that it had 'the bouquet of being employed by someone you went to boarding school with'. It's this sort of thing that makes people feel they can't enjoy wine, or worse, actively makes them despise it. What does an open can of tennis balls even smell like? I grew up near Wimbledon and even I don't know. You'd assume I was used to that smell. That every summer, the aroma of freshly opened cans of balls drifts across the common, filling the local nostrils with its distinctive scent. Let's not beat around the bush, I'm posh enough to have opened a can of tennis balls. Well, not once when I've done that have I exclaimed, 'This smells like a white wine!' (I also have no idea why they have to keep tennis balls in a sealed can, but that's a question for another book. Tuna I understand, but tennis balls?)

I've drunk wines that people describe as smelling of petrol. This, by the way, is apparently a positive thing to say. I don't mind the smell of petrol in the right context. However, the only right context for a petrol smell is a petrol station. That's where petrol lives. Even if you were in your car and you smelt petrol, that would be cause for concern. So, if I was to genuinely catch a whiff of it in my glass, that is going nowhere near my oesophagus. Americans don't even call it petrol. Does this mean that sommeliers in the US are all running around saying their Riesling smells like gas? That's very hard to make palatable.

It seems to me that quite a lot of wine language is unhelpfully creative, with experts trying to outdo each other with the weirdest and most original tasting note, regardless of whether the wine actually evokes it. I would draw the line at describing a wine as being adjacent to anything which I would not also want in my mouth. Otherwise, where does it end? As well as petrol, I've heard of wines that smell of wet grass, of manure, of slate and, most confusingly, of nail polish remover. These have all been aired in a positive context. I understand that there may be true wine buffs reading this now screaming at these pages, red and crusty lips flapping angrily. Probably something about how a wine can smell of something but not necessarily taste of it. But you know what? If I smell something bad, I don't want it in me. Humans have evolved to use their nose as the first line of defence.

Thankfully, whenever I've been told these aromas are present in a wine, I can't quite make them out. The petrol wine was delicious and tasted nothing like I'd just gone mouth to pump and taken a glug of premium unleaded. You should see this as a warning. If you ever come across one of these people, do not be thrown by their odd attempts to outfox you with bizarre descriptions of scent or flavour. Even better, beat them at their own game. Come up with your own offbeat comparisons. I guarantee these suggestions will impress them.

(A note: at the time of writing, I have not heard anyone use the words below. These wine nutters are constantly evolving though, so I have no doubt they will up their game and you will need to go even stranger. For now, these may help you out.)

'Fascinating . . . this pinot noir suggests blueberries, but the background rubber notes put me in mind of a punnet of blueberries that has been repeatedly run over by a moped. A Vespa GTS Super 300 if I'm not mistaken. With the additional floral bouquet, this moped is almost certainly being ridden by an attractive Italian nurse.'

'This is your classic watermelon that has been roundly told off.'

'You know that expensive coffee that weasels eat and then shit out and then they sell? It's like that, but with Chewits.'

'A can of tennis balls that was opened a year ago and then a dog has really had a go at the balls before they end up in a racist neighbour's garden for ages and you're too scared to go

and get them back because he hates the dog. In other words,
absolutely enchanting.'

'This is the unmistakeable aroma of a young boy's ambition.'

I fear the last few pages have been a vain attempt not to come across as a pretentious wine man. In all honesty, I have been pulled more and more in that direction of late. I am becoming everything I previously despised. I hesitate to call myself an oenophile (the term reserved for those truly dedicated to the cause) because my knowledge is minuscule. I also never want to be known as anything that ends in 'phile'. A certain type of criminal has really ruined that suffix for a lot of people. Isn't it horrible how a few rotten apples can ruin words for the rest of us?

I remember that during meals as a teenager I would sit and watch my dad (our family's resident wine expert) drink wine and find it totally laughable. Firstly, the glass swill. The glass swill is one of the most annoying flourishes of the wine drinker. They (we) will lie and say it's to aerate the wine, to get oxygen to it and enliven the flavour in the glass. It's been cooped up in that bottle for so long, it needs to be woken up from its hibernation! You know that bit in Disney's *Aladdin* when Robin Williams' Genie first explodes out of the lamp and has to stretch? ('Ten thousand years will give you such a crick in the neck!') Well, that's what they (we) will claim that they're (we're) doing. Cracking the Genie's neck. This is actually a much cooler name for it and may make it more acceptable.

'What are you doing, Dad?'

'I'm just cracking the Genie's neck, son!'

'Fair enough.'

I would try and get this phrase to take off, but thanks to the *Off Menu* podcast, my association with genies is already too strong.

The reason I am suspicious of the efficacy of this move is the frankly smug way in which they (we) do it. The little smile on the face of the swirler, staring into the glass and pretending that nobody else is watching, while secretly thinking that everyone is watching and thinks you are the sexiest person on the planet. The way they (we) act as if making liquid move around a glass is tantamount to something only a circus acrobat could pull off. Would this be an important thing to do if the action didn't seem to be so smooth and impressive? If tomorrow there was an announcement that it is actually more effective to oxygenate wine by honking into the bottle like a goose, would people do that? I suspect not. They would suddenly be very happy with the amount of air in the wine. Even after all this, I am disgusted to admit that I am now a swirler.

The bouquet we have broadly covered. I understand the principle, of course. We smell everything before we eat or drink it and a big ol' sniff can only enhance the experience of that first taste. What I don't understand is the long gap wine drinkers take between that smell and tasting it. The lengthy discussion, the comparing of notes. Or as it actually is, the dick-measuring competition. A protracted chat during which everybody tries to show off how much better their nose is than everybody else's. It's as if a group of drug sniffer dogs have been turned into humans by a witch and are struggling with normal small talk.

I may have accidentally made it sound much cuter than it is. It's actually very annoying. I think I resent this part of the process because of the size of my nose. It is impossibly tiny. Stop reading for a moment and check out the cover of this book.

You back? Mad small, isn't it? That same cheeky witch who transformed the dogs earlier was clearly present at my birth and cast a spell that made sure my nose didn't grow one bit from that day on. This witch, man. I don't understand the point of half of the stuff she's up to. She's also had a bloody go at my ears as well. Go back and check the cover.

Welcome back. See? I told you so. It's amazing the hurdles I've had to leap to get where I am today, what with my tiny nose and ears. I'm thankful never to have had a broken nose because I don't know what would be left. If this little button was pasted across my face, there would simply not be enough meat for it to recover. It would mean a lifetime of looking like Voldemort. Truthfully, it's not really an issue in most areas – unless one day I need spectacles. No way those things are staying on my face. So, the only problems they cause me are with glasses (eyes) and glasses (wine).

When I see everyone else smell a wine, they really get in there. My dad in particular has a honker to be admired. It's strong, looks trustworthy and could quite easily hit the bottom of a champagne flute if he so desired. It's the sort of schnozz that would look lovely in sculpture, and I, for one, am very jealous of it. I go through the rigmarole of smelling wine because I am that guy now. But there's honestly no point. My nose is so small that even when I ram my face right in there I'm barely smelling the liquid. In fact, I'm probably just picking up the scent of the room. I can try and add my thoughts to the nose chat, but chances are I'm smelling my own deodorant (Lynx Africa if I'm feeling saucy, Sure for Men if I'm looking to impress.)

The tasting should be the easy part. We've all tasted things before, right? Even a baby or a cat has tasted stuff, surely they can get involved with this aspect of wine appreciation? Wrong! Because when wine buffs taste, they (we) do not mean they put it in their mouth and then swallow it. They (we) *really* taste it. There is swilling around the mouth and even a bit where they (we) suck in air over the wine so it bubbles, clearly visible in your open gob to everyone else at the table. That's right, we're aerating again. Having just swirled, we're now swilling. This drink can't get enough bloody air, can it? It's a wonder they put it in a bottle in the first place. It feels quite cruel when you think about it. This wine that clearly loves air more than anything else is imprisoned in a bottle for years, sometimes decades. Then it finally tastes sweet oxygen and can truly be itself. It's swirled in a glass, having a whale of a time, then bubbled through a gob. It's like a day at a theme park for the wine. So much freedom! Then, without warning, it's swallowed and imprisoned again.

Then begins the arduous discussion of what people can taste. Whether any of this happens, of course, is based on what sort of social group you are with. I have two distinct groups of friends. One group is made up of wine people. We enjoy nothing more than sitting down with a few bottles and discussing their merits. Trust me when I tell you that even typing out that sentence fills me with a self-hatred that might require therapy. I, Ed Gamble, sit down with other people who like wine and we talk about the wine while drinking the wine. It's disgusting, really. It represents the ultimate lack of social skills, if you think about it. We get together once in a while and rather than discuss our lives, what we have been up to or the world at large, all we have to chat about is the drink that is right in front of us. What you are eating and drinking should really be, in any healthy social context, a complement to the evening itself. On these occasions, though, they *are* the evening. You may as well sit at home alone with a few bottles of wine, taste them and then check to see what other people on the internet said to see if what you thought matches up.

That is a specific example for a reason: I have also done this. I downloaded a wine app that includes user-sourced tasting notes. I will try a wine, jot down what I thought I could taste (blackberries, a winter walk, dirty nappies, etc.) and then check the app to see if people agreed. This sums me up. We've already discussed the true experts, those people who are desperate to stand out from the crowd with their outlandish descriptions of wine, but that is not for me. I want to know that I haven't got it wrong.

My wine friends will often say you can't get it wrong, that what you taste is what you taste, and nobody can deny that. That's an interesting philosophical point (finally, my degree comes in handy). We can never have privileged access to anyone else's internal experience, so how can we say what other people are tasting is wrong? For me, though, I like to *know* I am getting things right, and I need a pat on the back for doing so. I need a real and tangible score for everything, please and thank you. I don't much think about what happens after we die, but I like to imagine it's receiving your final score. An omniscient being will sit you down in a golden office and go through your life, decision by decision, and let you know what you did right and wrong before giving you your marks. From my calculations at the moment, I'm on about 55 per cent right. This is not bad for my age, but I have a lot of work to do, and I'll be starting with bringing up my wine-tasting mark.

My desperate need to fit in with people and have them agree with me has been a constant throughout my life. I don't know whether this is good or bad. What do you guys think? I'll just go along with that. This personality strength/flaw (depending on what you reckon) makes things like wine tasting an awkward event. I simultaneously want to be the one who says something clever but also gets everything correct. A typical inner monologue might go something like this . . .

This just tastes like wine to me. I can see that it's a red wine, shall I just say that it tastes red? There's no way anyone could disagree with that. But that isn't tasting, really, because you can see that with your eyes – eyes are not a mouth. I've heard people say you take the first taste with your eyes, but I don't think they mean that literally. No, think this through . . . I guess I can taste grapes. There are almost certainly grapes in here, if I know wine. Come to think of it, I've never once heard any of these so-called experts say that a wine tastes like grapes. If I say 'grapes', will I be hailed as a hero? Or is that so obvious that nobody ever says it? That's a risk I'm not willing to take. Maybe I should say it tastes like Marmite? That would be bold, because it definitely doesn't taste like Marmite. Who are they to say I can't taste Marmite though? But what if they tell me off? I don't want to be told off . . .

That final thought is the boiled-down essence of much of my personality. My greatest fear is being told off. Every single social situation or new employment opportunity is played through in my head before I enter into it. The possible good outcomes are dispatched quickly so that I can get to imagining the worst-case scenario as soon as possible. I really like to get my mind-teeth into potential disasters. For many people, their greatest fear is death. If these people are imagining the worst thing that could possibly happen, it inevitably ends with their death or the death of a loved one. This is not a thought that plagues me. (I'd rather not die, sure, though at least I would find out my score.) Death rarely pops up in my frequent mental doom scrolling. Instead, it normally involves being told off and being banished from a room. I can't think of anything worse than being in a social situation and saying something innocuous which causes everyone else in the room to go silent and stare at you, before they all pile on to reprimand you. The very idea of it fills me with the icy dread that most people reserve for the end of a life. Remember that scene in *Goodfellas* where Joe Pesci's character is laughing then suddenly switches to being terrifyingly angry? Imagine that scene, but everyone around you does it at the same time. That's what I play out every time I do a dry run of anything in my head.

Even worse, what if everyone laughs at you? This may seem like an odd thing for a comedian to worry about. Surely making everyone laugh is the ideal situation for someone who is essentially a clown? It's important to distinguish between *types* of laughter. As a comedian, I want people to laugh at things I say that I have machine-tooled in order to make them laugh. It's all about intention. I am a comedian because my worst fear is people laughing *at* me for things that I did not intend to be funny (serious opinions, my genuine personality, body shape, etc.). My only way of stopping this is to control the laughter. My entire job is in response to my preposterous fear that people are laughing at me behind my back.

Even if I wasn't intending to be funny, being a comedian is a great get-out clause. Here is a perfect example. I was at the wedding of some of my wife's friends recently. We are all friends, sure, but they were my wife's friends first. When there is an extra link in a friendship you still need to be on your social guard. It's still possible to embarrass yourself beyond repair in front of these people in a way that's much harder to do in front of your direct friends. So, I was on my best wedding behaviour. I wanted to make a good impression, or, ideally for my personality, absolutely no impression at all. To sink into the crowd, be part of their special day but a part that nobody notices, like brushstrokes on a painting. Texture. At a direct friend's wedding, I'm a very different guy. Fill me with champagne, I'll heckle the speeches, request the DJ play Limp Bizkit and breakdance until it's time to be dragged home. Not on that day though.

I didn't avoid the champagne (that would've made me stand out even more), but I didn't have enough to give me any outlandish confidence. I looked nice (but not too nice) and was doing a great job chatting with the assembled throng. I kept my conversation topics to the beige and standard – 'What a lovely day', 'They must be so happy', 'Great vows', etc. I was doing well. Then the time came to sit down at the table.

I don't mean to show off, but this is something I've done before. Loads of times, in fact. I must by now be well into five figures for the number of times I've sat down in chairs. I'm sitting down right now, as a matter of fact, and let me tell you, I've nailed it. As I sat down at this wedding, though, it immediately became clear something was wrong. This was not like other times I had sat down. I thought to myself, 'This wooden chair feels a little rickety, how curious, I hope it—' and at that point the chair completely shattered beneath me. And I mean *shattered*. Not just into its constituent parts (legs, seat, back) but into a pile of firewood that most people would struggle to work out had even started life as a chair. I couldn't have done a better job if I'd taken a hatchet to it. But I hadn't taken a hatchet to it, I'd taken my arse to it.

I hit the floor with an audible thud and everyone around my table and on the surrounding tables stopped and looked. There were a few gasps of shock. This was true nightmare fuel. I found myself at a crossroads. Do I follow my instincts, pick myself up and run out of the room before throwing my phone in the sea, leaving my wife and moving to a place where news of my chair destruction hadn't yet reached? Every single cell of my body wanted to throw a strop. As a formerly larger man, the sort of embarrassment you feel when something like this happens is sharp and deep. If I'd been one of those lifelong slim and confident people, I might not have felt this way. As someone who spent his formative years as a chubster, however, I was mortified. Yet again I was playing out the next seconds in my head and imagining other guests' inner monologues. 'Gosh, he must be heavy,' they were surely all thinking. 'Who's the tubber who just smashed up this wonderful day with his fat butt?' they were saying (with their eyes).

This is where being a comedian is a wonderful get-out clause. I could control people's reactions. I laughed it off. It took me a long time to learn this lesson, but laughing things off is often the best course of action. It's also what most people expect from a comic. In reality the majority of us are fragile husks, but most people assume we are fun-loving guys who are up for a laugh one hundred per cent of the time. In this instance, I reacted almost like I had meant to do it. I posed for photos with the broken chair, cackling away as if I had actually added another fantastic memory to this glorious day. I even posted it to Instagram. When a member of staff had to go and fetch me a spare chair (which was of course noticeably different from the rest of them), I made jokes about that too. I forced myself to be a laugh on my own terms and it made the day infinitely better. I'm not saying the photos of the chair made the wedding album, but I'm happy it didn't end in tears.

So in a wine-tasting situation I try to go with the crowd. It's easier that way. It's also preferable to go with the crowd when the people you're with don't care about wine. I will switch my personality immediately. There will be no attempt to recognize flavours or smells, just straight glugging. Even worse, I will join in slagging off people who do enjoy wine in this way. I'll call them pretentious and verbose, I'll describe them as toffs with nothing better to do, all the while fully aware that I am living a double life.

In many ways, my life is that of a superhero, albeit a very tedious superhero. By day, I am a regular man drinking lager and supermarket wine, without a care for the bouquet or legs. I will swig on a Guinness, do a big burp and then cheer when someone drops a tray. But by night I become . . . Wine-Wanker. My equivalent of the Batcave (Wankcave) is one of those restaurants where they bring tiny portion after tiny portion of food, each with its own wine, and I will sit and swill and swirl to my heart's content. I will listen to the sommelier, desperately trying to absorb titbits of information about the different wines that I can later casually pass off in conversation as if I've known them for years.

The more I write, the less this sounds like a superhero alter ego. Because Ed and WineWanker are not two separate but equal personalities that I can switch between easily, like Bruce Wayne seems to. The older I get, the more I find myself being dragged into WineWanker's dark and murky world. The other night we had friends over for dinner – friends who are not interested in wine over and above the fact that it tastes nice (as it should be). I proudly announced that I had two vintages of the same wine and it would be fun to see what the differences were and which we preferred. FUN. I MEANT THAT. The bleed through my personas has begun. If I am a superhero, I am one of the ones that gets bitten by a radioactive creature and slowly turns into them. In this case, I have clearly been bitten by a radioactive dad.

My dad has many qualities that I admire and would gladly welcome. He is a hugely intelligent and hard-working man with an insatiable passion for history and literature. Frustratingly, these are not the aspects of his personality I have absorbed. I wilfully act like a moron for money, in a profession that affords me a lot of free time which I treat as mini holidays. I can barely remember what happened yesterday, let alone what happened in the Russian Revolution.

No, these are not the parts of my father I have chosen to adopt. I have started to transition some of my habits into some of his worst, most pretentious characteristics. Nothing illustrates this more than wine. As I said, I used to scoff at him and his friends for sitting round the dinner table discussing the finer merits of a Chablis. I would tuck into a refreshing Diet Coke and chuckle to myself (and also loudly in their posturing faces). I'll never drink anything other than DC, I would think to myself. DC is reliable, DC is always the same.

You don't have to discuss or argue about loyal ol' DC! These people are ridiculous, I would think (and also tell them to their posturing faces). I don't remember a particular moment when I started turning into my dad. It sneaks up on you as a man after you turn thirty. One day you're sniggering at the things they do, the next you find yourself doing them.

In many areas, I have had a complete personality change in the last few years of my life. I used to be the most chaotically messy person. I've already divulged a lot of what my life was like at university. It will not surprise you that I lived in absolute filth. For three years I happily existed among piles of dirty clothes, plates caked with old food and the odd rat. In my house share in the second year, we found a frog in the kitchen. The back door was shut, as were all the windows. Quite how the frog got in there was a total *Jonathan Creek*-style mystery. Unlike Jonathan Creek, though, I was unable to come up with a solution within the hour. My only guess is that it somehow mutated from a dirty old pasta plate that had been left there for a fortnight. Perhaps we accidentally discovered some sort of new breeding technique. Tomato and basil + time = amphibian life. As soon as I saw it, I bundled it up into a crusty tea towel, chased my housemate Kat around the house with it, and then gently put it in the garden. It then presumably had to try and integrate with other frogs and attempt to explain why it stank of Loyd Grossman sauce. Even living in this *Life of Grime* level of mess, though, I was happy.

At the end of my first year, my mum came to pick me up to take me home and clear out my room. Despite my protestations, she opened my wardrobe. From the top shelf came tumbling every single item of unwashed clothing that I'd accrued in the months of living there. I can't stress this enough: this was *every* item of clothing I owned (minus what I was wearing – we're not that sort of family). Going to university is supposed to be a time for progression, when you learn to live without the constant life support of a parent. I had instead regressed to the life of a caveman. (Although that's actually doing a disservice to cavemen. They only had one or two pairs of little fur pants and I'm sure they regularly used to beat those bad boys against a river rock.) Together we stuffed everything into bin bags and left for London. I looked like I had just got out of prison.

I don't know when I made the sudden switch to my current fastidiousness, but it was swift. The first time I noticed it was when I started flat sharing in London with the comedian and feral hound Nish Kumar. It was an exciting time. Two best buds in their mid-twenties, both starting out in comedy and sharing laughs, lodgings and lagers. What became immediately evident, though, was that I had suddenly made a lurch towards the sort of house pride my father was famous for. One night, after we had finished another marathon *Pointless* session, Nish went to bed. I, however, had other plans. I had to stay up and *plump the sofa cushions*. This is not something I remember starting to do in my life; like all my other personality shifts, it snuck up on me. There I was, a man who had recently been perfectly happy to drop spaghetti down the back of the sofa and leave it there, *plumping cushions*. I even karate-chopped the top of them because I'd seen someone do it in a documentary about a posh hotel. This is exactly the sort of thing my dad would do. The transformation had begun in earnest. From then on it was a slippery slope to today's Ed swirling wine and having to be right in conversations.

What happened to that messy guy who thought that sitting on an unplumped sofa was EXACTLY THE SAME as sitting on a plumped one? Well, he's gone, and he's never coming back. There are some benefits, of course. I get on much better with my dad now, primarily because we are slowly becoming the same person. He's not becoming more like me, I should say. It's a very one-sided transaction. He's not budging.

My life has been replete with these sorts of transformations. From my fastidiousness to my weight and damn near my entire personality, I have been through a lot of unexpected changes. When we're younger, we tend to think we are set in stone. We can't foresee a time when we will be any different. I almost stubbornly resisted any shift in my lifestyle or attitude, thinking any evolution would somehow be letting my former self down. I now see that these kinds of changes are natural and necessary – if I'd refused to alter who I was when I was in my early twenties, I imagine my loved ones would be quite worried about me at this point. I would be extremely unhealthy, living in filth and, quite frankly, I'd probably stink. I would also be perpetually single, the idea of romance remaining a concept. Because as we're about to discover, my past is not exactly littered with sexual escapades.

8

NOODLES AND SNOGGING

If music be the food of love, play on.

I've never really understood this quote. As someone who has always been very food-focused, I could never get to grips with why 'food' is buried in the middle, assisting a metaphor that thrusts 'music' and 'love' to the forefront. I enjoy music, sure. Love's nice, I guess. But food has always been the overarching thing in my life. Wee Willy Shakespeare clearly didn't agree. He was obviously too busy writing his plays to enjoy food. I suspect he was a Fueller. For me, a better version of this line would be 'If food be the food of food, eat on.' This might not make as much sense or be as poetic, but it says all I need it to.

I had intended this chapter to be a whirlwind journey through my romantic history via the medium of food. On reviewing my romantic history, though, I have concluded that it would be a very short chapter. I don't know whose life I was originally thinking of, but it certainly wasn't mine. I was always one step behind at school when it came to things like that. Much like when I was surprised when everyone started drinking, when I found out that some of the boys had started kissing girls, I was shocked. Nobody had told me this was the plan. If I'd known, I could've prepared! I could've started practising! Quite how I would've practised, I don't know. Teenagers are often depicted as trying out their kissing technique on oranges, but I would've just eaten the orange. This, I'm sure you can agree, is not the best training for your first kiss. The last thing anyone wants from a snogging partner is someone who tries to peel your lips.

What I really needed to do first was practise talking to girls, which was almost impossible, as I went to an all-boys school. This is just one of many reasons why these institutions are completely out of date and unhelpful. It's baffling to see quite how they ever thought it would prepare us for the outside world because – I don't know if you know this – there are women in the outside world. But from the age of eleven to eighteen, five days a week, eight hours a day, I exclusively socialized with people of my own sex. Meaning that when the time finally came to interact with girls, I had no idea what to do. Luckily, the girls that we started hanging out with were from all-girls schools, meaning that they had even less of an idea how to interact with us. Those parties were basically two races of aliens attempting to establish a galaxy peace accord.

But, before I knew it, romantic connections were being made. This makes it sound a bit more period drama than it was. As is traditional, these 'romantic connections' were mainly made up of sloppy and awkward lip fights, usually in the middle of a party while everyone cheered. I must stress, I was never one of the combatants in the lip skirmishes. I was a cheerer, and perfectly happy with this for a good while. What can I say? I support my friends. They're having some lovely kisses – good for them. I'll bide my time, I thought. My friends have had their turn, surely it'll be mine soon.

But by the time I decided it was my turn, all the girls were my friends as well. I was friend-zoned by everyone. This is not a bad thing, in my opinion. For too long, the friend zone has been heralded as a negative thing – the worst place someone can be. Imagine, though, if you used the term with someone who had never heard it before. The friend zone. It sounds amazing, doesn't it? The best and safest place that one can be. If there was a friend zone in the Crystal Maze, that would be the best one. It's the opposite of a war zone, and I was perfectly happy to be there.

If you're a young person who worries that they may be permanently in the friend zone, there are some clues you might want to look out for. I know all of these from experience. These are all things that have happened to me, and while at the time they may have stung, I came to realize that in the long game, I probably should've taken them as compliments.

1. If anyone you might be romantically interested in comes to you privately to ask you for advice about

being in love with one of your friends, your goose is cooked. You are in the friend zone, buddy. You are a trusted confidant, and being a confidant does not mix with a future fling. A shoulder to cry on is never connected to some lips to kiss on. And don't think that if you reject being a confidant this somehow puts you in a better position. You will just come across as a prick. Be a nice person and go home and practise on your orange some more.

2. If a group of people you might be romantically interested in publicly declares you their 'favourite' of the group that they might be romantically interested in, you are done for. They may as well putty over your genitals and start keeping you as a pet. Again, don't resist this. You just have more friends now. As long as you know that there is literally no chance of any sexual encounters, just let it happen. It's nice to be someone's favourite!

3. If someone you are convinced you are in love with says 'You're so nice, I can see myself marrying you when I'm forty,' you may as well get on a boat and live on the boat. This happened to me as a teenager on more than one occasion. The first time, I'm ashamed to say, I took it as a sign that maybe they were interested. I ignored all the key red flags in that sentence, like 'nice', 'marrying' and 'forty'. Forty is probably the major burn here, and both times I was told this, they were very specific about

forty. If you were thirty-eight when you were told this, you could probably see it as a positive. Aged sixteen, not so much. I can't stress enough, they don't mean this, so please don't message them at one minute past midnight on your fortieth birthday.

What you come to realize as a teenager is that nobody is really interested in 'nice' or 'friendly'. These are not exciting qualities in a potential short-term romance when you are in your youth. This absolutely does not mean, though, that you should not be these things. Embrace them headlong, because in the long term you will discover that these qualities will become an absolute commodity. These are things that people value once they've got all that other stuff out of their systems. This is not to say that my teen years were completely without any frissons whatsoever. I had the occasional drunken kiss at a party, but they did not tend to go hugely well. I won't go into details here, but if a person you've just kissed immediately then vomits in a sink, it's difficult to count that as a win.

When I left school, I wasn't exactly primed to be sexually successful at university. I had taken on the role of fat best friend with aplomb and that is a role that is terrifically hard to break out of. University is a great opportunity to change your personality. It's a new set of people who have no idea what your social role was up until that point – you have a chance to reinvent yourself completely and start again. This, however, is easier said than done. As much as

I may have hoped that I could arrive on campus and immediately establish myself as some sort of magnificent shagger, this was not to be. I quickly fell back into my position as trusted friend and sexless confidant. I had designs on becoming some sort of mysterious Byron-type figure, wending my way round college and sleeping with woman after woman, leaving them gasping and spreading rumours among their friends of this incredible man. In many ways I was a Byron-type figure already, but the Byron in question was Byron Burgers, which had greatly contributed to my figure.

Women love mystery, I thought. Surely I can be mysterious at university? But mystery, as I found out, is a very hard trait to learn. How do you suddenly become mysterious? Now I think it's a quality people are just naturally born with. It's a delicate balance; there's a fine line between 'mysterious' and 'creepy'. Do you start hiding round corners? Living in the shadows? Do you just start not giving too much away? Maybe when someone asks you your name, you just look darkly at them and say, 'I don't have a name.' Is that mysterious, or just weird? The particular brand of mystery I decided to go with was perhaps too advanced. I just decided to stay in my room most of the time. I was the ultimate mystery. I forgot, of course, that you had to be mysterious to people while also not being completely absent from all social events. There's a difference between women saying, 'Oh my God, who's THAT guy?' and saying, 'Seriously, who *is* that guy? I've never seen him before and first year is nearly over.'

It's not like I didn't try to make connections with people. It was the first time I had been outside the bubble of school for over a decade, and I was nervous about making new friends, let alone meeting anyone who was more than a friend. I even followed some of my mum's advice – the absolute kiss of death. I wanted to be the new cool guy at uni, and I turned up armed with social tools, as an eighteen-year-old man, that my mum had given me. I think I was aware that this was tragic at the time, but I was willing to try anything. I turned up stinking of desperation.

The advice went thusly. As soon as I arrived in my halls of residence, I was to set up my kettle, boil it and make myself a cup of tea. Crucially, I was to do this with my door propped open. The aim? That someone on my corridor would be wandering past, see what I was doing and stick their head in. Then, all casual like, I would say, 'Hi, I'm Ed, nice to meet you! I was just making a cup of tea, do you want one?' Bang, I'd make a friend. Presumably then word would spread, and before I knew it I would have a queue outside my room of fellow students desperate for a cuppa and a natter with this charming new pal.

You'll be amazed to hear that this is not how it went down. I arrived earlier than most people, so the building was deserted. This was already an obstacle, but I had promised my mum I would try. The first cup of tea ensnared nobody in my net. I didn't drink tea, so that went down the sink almost immediately. I boiled the kettle a few more times, hoping that the bubbling would at least catch someone's attention. Eventually, just when I'd given up hope, it did. A head poked around the door, just as Mummy had promised. Unfortunately, it was the head of a janitor, who wanted to know if he could change a lightbulb. Needs must, I thought, and that janitor is still my best friend to this day. (He's not, of course. Lovely man, but he didn't seem interested in going to fresher events with me because he was in his forties and married with kids. I didn't get a chance to ask him if he married his childhood sweetheart aged forty because of a promise she made, he just packed up his little toolbox and left.) I made a few more cups of tea (straight down the sink) and gave up.

Please don't feel sorry for me, I eventually found my tribe. I threw myself into making sketch comedy with trusted friends and had the time of my life. I found what I wanted to do with my life, and you can't ask for much more than that. None of this was helpful with my love life, though. I can't imagine it's hugely alluring to women to see a young man constantly in the college bar writing fart jokes with some other silly boys. As much as I love Nish Kumar, who was at Durham with me, we weren't exactly the dream team when it came to attracting the opposite sex. We were wingmen without a plane.

Not that I could say we ever really actively tried. We found our romantic failures objectively hilarious and almost egged each other on to be even more useless. We had a good gang of friends in the sketch group. It was me, Nish, Tom Neenan and Pete Riley. I've left mentioning Tom and Pete until now because they had the temerity to step outside the group and actually have some success with women. Scabs. No wonder Nish and I weren't able to work our magic. We would spend most of our time together and would always be the last ones alone in the pub. We branded ourselves the 'One More Boys', due to our habit of always having one more drink. That feels even more pathetic to write down than it does to remember it. We liked to imagine, I think, that we were members of an exclusive club that everyone wanted in on. In our minds, all the other students were watching us from the other side of the room thinking, 'God, I wish I could have a drink with the One More Boys. They're so funny and sexy, but I couldn't possibly approach them!' In reality we were quite invisible, while everyone else got on with meeting new people and having casual sex. I wouldn't trade it for the world though, and when I'm forty I will marry Nish.

THE TOP THREE WORST FOODS TO EAT ON A DATE (THAT I WISH I'D KNOWN AT THE TIME)

Noodles

This one is particularly painful for me. When I first started dating my wife, I thought it would be a wonderful idea to take her to Wagamama's. I now know that this was a terrible plan. For a start, you have to sit on bench seating, rammed in with other people. They are all within earshot and love to eavesdrop when they pick up on the vibe that they are next to people making their first tentative steps into a relationship. I know this because I have done it. You are sat so close to people that conversation between you is impossible. Your radar is constantly trained on the lives of other people.

Wagamama's also insist on bringing out the food whenever it is ready. The waiting staff proudly tell you this when you sit down, as if it is a plus point in their ethos. For someone who gets real food anxiety in restaurant situations like I do, this is a nightmare. I am always worried that they have forgotten dishes or they're going to come at the wrong time. Where does it end? Does this give them licence to bring the pudding first and the starters with the bill? Wagamama's is a lawless society and must be stopped at all costs. I sat there, leg bouncing nervously, as other people got their dishes plonked in front of them so close to us that we could smell them. Not a great energy for a date.

But the main thing that makes it a bad date spot is the noodles. There is no sexy way to eat noodles. I remember early dates there, my wife and I both shielding our mouths to disguise the fact that we had long wet strands hanging out of them. I doubt either of us would've been put off each other by this sight, but you just don't know that in the early days. You assume that the other person will be disgusted if they look up from their ramen and see Doctor Zoidberg across the table. This also goes for spaghetti, by the way, if you thought I am unfairly focusing on Asian cuisine. I honestly do not know how the Lady and the Tramp ever continued that relationship. Some of you might see that scene where they suck a spaghetti strand down together as romantic. To me, that is a horror movie.

Soup

Soup is bad on dates for a couple of reasons. Firstly, the slurp factor. In fact, anyone who can eat soup in public full stop is clearly a sociopathic maniac. I've tried eating it quietly, but I simply find it impossible. Every single spoonful makes me sound like a bog monster, and I am in favour of making it illegal to serve it in restaurants. By all means eat soup in the privacy of your own home, but do not inflict it on others.

There may be some people who claim to be able to eat soup quietly and think that I just have bad table manners. To those people I say, watching you desperately try to eat soup quietly is even more embarrassing than witnessing a slurper. The way you slowly lift the spoon to your mouth and delicately place your lips on the spoon . . . horrible. And if, during this process, you happen to clink one of your teeth on the spoon? You should be in prison, where your habits will get even shorter shrift. One tooth clink in the canteen and the other prisoners will have no choice but to take their own spoons and shank you to death with them.

I am not put off by much on a date, but if someone ordered soup I might think twice about seeing them again. Slurping aside, the lack of ambition that this action represents is astounding. Out of everything available, you choose soup? I'm sorry, are you a baby? Because that's what soup is. Baby food. There's no difference. Nice ingredients have been taken and needlessly blended and mashed together, creating a liquid mush to soothe your little baby gums. You've ordered a steak for mains – would you feel more comfortable if we popped that in a blender as well? Maybe you should drink your steak too, you tiny little child. The only people who should be allowed to eat soup are those with false teeth or prospectors in a gold rush who have to cook on an open fire. Safe to say, I have never dated anyone from either of these groups.

Oysters

The reputation of oysters is that they are an aphrodisiac, and I can't for the life of me work out why. Apparently, the mere act of eating an oyster causes a physical reaction that increases sexual desire. I've personally never felt this when I've had an oyster. Now that I've looked it up, it seems they contain zinc, which is a nutrient that increases testosterone production and spermatogenesis. Not so sexy now, hey? I would say that if you are having oysters on a date because you think they are an aphrodisiac, please do not try and explain the science. The last word a potential partner wants to hear is 'spermatogenesis'.

Perhaps, as oysters are expensive, they are a flex because it shows you are willing to splash the cash? Well, if you're dating someone who is impressed by this, please stop it. Nothing good lies down that path.

The main issues with oysters are essentially the same as the problem with soup or noodles. There is no cool way to eat them. Watching someone eat oysters is, in my opinion, the antithesis of a turn-on. To successfully dispatch one, you have to slurp. There's no other way. But you might find that the oyster doesn't give in so easily. It might be slightly stuck to the shell, leaving you to slurp endlessly, before having to grab a little fork and pry it away, only to slurp again. If there's anything less attractive than a slurp at the dinner table, it's an extended and unsuccessful slurp.

Having said all this, maybe if you're looking for a long-term partner, it might be best to lay all your habits on the table, literally. We all slurp in our private lives, why disguise that during our first interactions with people? Maybe we should just be honest and let them know what they're in for. Suck the noodles, glug the soup and slurp the oysters. This will save you a lot of hassle later down the line when you have to reveal your true self. At that point, you have to admit to them that the version of yourself you presented early on was a lie.

Dating on the whole is a lie. We are all catfish. I have friends who point-blank refuse to fart in front of a partner, even years into a relationship. They will do all they can never to break wind near the person they claim to love, to the point of painful stomach complaints. Perhaps initially I understand this. You want to get to know someone before you unleash your true butt personality. But really, if you're doing this a month in, who are you kidding? Are you trying to pretend to them that you don't fart? If I went out with someone and suspected that they didn't fart, it would actually be a turn-off and a medical worry. Just relax and let rip. It's cute. It's just something else you can share. It's also a natural by-product of eating out together, which is a must for me. If you want to explore the varied world of cuisine, you also have to admit to yourself that you will also be exploring the varied world of guffs. If they don't want to join you on this journey, then that's their loss and they can go and find a partner who never farts, like a cyborg. As I always say: if food is the food of love, fart on. So let's just all agree not to lie to any prospective partners, shall we? Promise me, on your next date you will arrive, slurp some noodles, gulp an oyster and then fart the loudest fart you can possibly muster. If they look disgusted, they are not the one for you.

When I started going out with Charlie (wife), I was evidently very inexperienced in the dating field. My lack of success in relationships (or more realistically, my lack of relationships full stop) had left me quite downhearted and feeling like perhaps it just wasn't for me. Maybe I would be one of those people who don't have romance in their lives. And you know what? That probably would've been fine. You don't pine after what you haven't had, and I had become perfectly comfortable with being outside that world.

I suppose I was an incel, in a way, but a happy one. You never hear about those guys. All the incels (involuntary celibates, Grandad) we hear about these days are so angry!

They hate the fact that they are not sexually active, and they have decided to focus that anger on the women they think should be sleeping with them. I must say that I was not one of them. I had accepted my lot. They all seem to live in their mum's basement and spend all day online. I did live with my mum, but she did not have a basement and the internet was shaky to say the least. It's very difficult to rage against women on forums if your mum is in the next room and you can't get online if she is on the phone.

So, to meet Charlie was a surprise. A nice one, I should add. Like a fiver-in-an-old-jacket surprise, rather than a birthmark-you-didn't-know-about surprise. I wasn't expecting anything to come from us meeting, given my previous experiences. My eating and weight were out of control, and as much as it shouldn't have been an issue, it definitely dented my confidence. It had affected me in my interactions with women in the past. I had it in my head that the reason I was so often relegated to the friend zone was because of my size. This, I think now, couldn't have been further from the truth. Maybe when you're a teenager, aesthetics mean more, but you cannot underestimate the importance of confidence. I know plenty of bigger people who are comfortable in their own skin to the extent that their confidence beams out of them in a hugely attractive way. This, however, is not something I had. I was loud, yes. People thought I was funny for the most part. But it was always very obvious that I was doing all of these things to paper over cracks in my self-worth, which is not an attractive quality. I even went through an even less attractive phase of wearing bold and ridiculous clothes in an attempt to deflect from my perceived flaws. This would surely work, I thought. How would people notice my size if they were too busy marvelling at my bright blue and pink clothes? I leaned into the sort of outfits that you would expect to see an American dad wear at Disneyland. Safe to say, this didn't improve my chances with women.

When I met Charlie, I went into it in the way I always had. Open-hearted and friendly with absolutely no expectations of her liking me in that way. It turns out, that finally paid off. Remember when I told you being nice is a commodity eventually? Well, I am living proof. It took a while, but it happened. A lot of people assume I met Charlie after I had lost weight, got on top of my health and sorted my life out. Well, no. When Charlie met me, I was perhaps at the nadir of my wellbeing and self-confidence. Shrewd move on her part, I guess. Touché, wife. She'd obviously scoured the country for the most broken men whom she thought had the most potential to improve. She settled on me, and I couldn't have been more delighted.

I should also say at this stage that my lifestyle change and self-improvement were not driven by her in any way. I think some people may have suspected that at the time. I finally started going out with someone, and then immediately began trying to lose weight. It looks fishy from the outside. As if she were some sort of evil stepmom from a 1990s movie giving me an ultimatum. This couldn't be further from the truth, though. My actions were completely driven by my own ego. Charlie has always been very clear that she doesn't mind what I look like. That's the great thing: she started seeing me when I was fat and has been with me through all my changes. She's always very careful never to say that she prefers me any particular way, that she is just happy if I am. This is both proof that she actually loves me for me and, as I see it, an absolute licence to stack it all back on when I'm fifty.

This does not mean that she fully supports me in all my current foodie endeavours. If anything, she finds my obsession mildly annoying. When we first started seeing each other, I didn't really care what I ate, just as long as there was a huge amount of it. There's a certain degree of freedom in this. You don't have to spend hours examining menus on a restaurant's website, reading reviews or asking for recommendations. Dinner is dinner, whether you are in an acclaimed Michelin-starred eatery or you've just nipped to the petrol station. This was what it was like when we were first getting to know each other in the early years. We would sit in my mum's house chatting and laughing, perfectly happy just to eat crisps and mini Battenberg cakes for lunch. Charlie loved this . . . I think. She is, and always has been, a snacker. Snacks can constitute an entire meal for her. Even now, when I go away on tour, I will come back and no real shopping has been done. There is just a fridge full of pickles, which she will nibble on throughout the day at indiscriminate times before going to bed having had nothing substantial.

I have never subscribed to this way of living. I love a snack, don't misunderstand me. Nuts, especially, are one of my true loves. I will gobble handfuls of them like some sort of squirrel king, piling in fistful after fistful until my mouth is stinging with salt. But this would never replace a meal. Even if I'm full to the brim with snacks, I cannot miss the main event. I need my three solid meals a day, otherwise I feel like I have somehow been cheated. Even on Christmas Day, when lunch is so impossibly massive that by the time 10 p.m. rolls around you still feel like you could never eat again, I still squeeze in another meal. There is absolutely no physical desire to, but I have a burning psychological need. Why should I go to bed with only two meals onboard? Who am I, a workhouse orphan? No, I am Mr Bumble, and Mr Bumble needs dinner.

The early days of our relationship suited Charlie down to the ground where food was concerned. We would snack all day and I could still fit in my meals. Bliss for all concerned. After I lost weight, however, my true foodie instincts kicked in. Partly, I think, because for the first time in my life I felt hunger. Before then, I had always been full. Once I tried to eat in a more ordered way, I felt actual hunger for the first time, especially when I first started. My stomach went from having pounds upon kilos of food piled into it to welcoming what was a wholly more normal quantity. As such, it would spend most of the day screaming and rumbling at me in sheer shock. In order to combat this, I would spend hours watching food shows and reading restaurant blogs. I started to become fascinated with all things culinary and was determined to explore the world through food. There's no nicer way of putting this: I became a complete food wanker. I still am.

Charlie, on the other hand, is not. She enjoys good food, but it is not her sole driving purpose in life. She values trifling things like 'social events'. She will happily go to a nice restaurant with friends and enjoy the company as much as the food. Personally, I would have a much better time completely alone, away from the prying eyes of others so I can ask the waiter annoying questions like where the duck is from and which tennis-ball wine pairs best with it. I truly believe that if Charlie had met me when I was in this phase, the ick she would've experienced would've put her off even a second date. There is a huge list of food-based habits I have that make her roll her eyes, and here are just a few of them. Maybe you can imagine having to sit opposite this at a table and decide whether you would leave me or not.

Refusing to talk about anything other than the food while we are eating the food

Many of you may see a meal in a restaurant as a chance to catch up on your day and discuss a wide range of topics. Well, you are wrong. Idle chit-chat is for the way to the restaurant and the way home from the restaurant. While you are on the hallowed turf, all I want to discuss is the food we are about to eat, currently eating or have just finished eating. Why would we talk about anything else? There is so much to cover! The way the food has been cooked, the flavour profiles, comparisons with other places we have been. I will allow some discussion about the layout of the dining room, but this is only permitted until the menus are brought over.

I will not eat and walk at the same time

Sometimes we will be in a rush to get to something which is not food-focused (almost always Charlie's choice). In these instances she will often suggest just 'grabbing a quick bite' and eating it while we walk. This is a hard pass for me. It's a waste of a meal. Food is designed to be savoured, enjoyed, to be the absolute main focal point of an evening. All other events are peripheral. I can't think of anything worse than trying to eat something while also concentrating on walking in a straight line. The walking will inevitably suffer, and I will end up in the road. I would much rather have a full sit-down meal and miss the first part of whatever we are going to, be it a film or a funeral.

I will be tense until our order is taken

This is a bad one. I should clarify that I am never rude or short with waiters. If you are the sort of person who is ever snappy or downright abusive to servers, please close this book and hit yourself over the head with it. No matter how disastrous a night a restaurant may be having, it is almost certainly not the fault of the person out front. There will be plenty of people being rude, so please just be the nice table they have that night. I am, however, not fun to be around until I have ordered. I will be stiff, tense and anxious until I know for sure that our order is winging its way to the kitchen. As soon as a waiter has approached our table for the first time, my wife can see me visibly relax. Fun guy to marry, right? (This doesn't go for Wagamama's, of course. There's no guarantee that ordering means any-thing in that chaotic Wild West of a restaurant.)

I will not order the same as anyone else at the table

This is a big one. All the other habits, I admit, can be annoying. This is the one that I simply don't understand other people disagreeing with. If I am in a restaurant and someone orders the same dish as I want before I get a chance to order, I will change my order regardless of whether I want the alternative or not. If I order before them and they try to order the same, I will try my hardest to con-vince them to get something else. If this fails, we return to the previous plan and I change my order. I simply see no point in anyone ordering the same thing, especially if we are visiting a specific restaurant for the first time. What are we there for, if not to explore the full breadth of the menu on offer?

Many people worry about food envy when they see their companion's dishes arrive. This is not something I'm con-cerned with, so confident am I that I will order the right thing. Envy creeps in, however, when I believe that the table has not ordered enough of the menu. I am envious of dishes that have not been made and left in the kitchen, destined never to fulfil their full potential of being eaten by us. Let's have a bit of ambition, people. Let's all order different things.

Food noises

Yes, most people would find this annoying. If I eat something I like, I will make noises verging on the orgasmic. Usually these will just be grunts and moans, but sometimes I will manage to form phrases like 'Oh God' or 'Yes please,' and in rare circumstances I will go beyond words, and start to wriggle around in my seat and do a little happy dance. This annoys my wife to such an extent that I can practically see her mentally drafting divorce papers. Fair enough. If you heard someone you didn't know doing this in a public place, you'd be disgusted. Well, imagine being legally bound to this person. You'd seriously question your life choices.

Those are my top picks, but like I say, the list of my annoying food behaviours is endless. For the purposes of this book, I asked Charlie what bothers her most about me in a food setting. She was far too quick to respond (with a voice note, to make sure I could really hear the disdain). She didn't classify or divide them into neat little categories like

I just have, but it's worth me relaying what she said so you can be in no doubt quite how annoyingly my food obsession manifests itself.

> When we are eating in a restaurant you'll say something like 'Oh, I can really taste the bergamot in this, can't you?', but you don't actually want to know what I think, you just want to say that you can taste bergamot and get a pat on the back.
>
> When the meal arrives, you're like 'oh', as if you need some silence for the dish like we're in a weird church, but we're not. It's a dinner.

Food can be a wonderful thing for relationships. Meals can mark pivotal moments in love, creating a sensory memory that makes the whole thing seem more evocative when you look back. 'Remember our first date – we ate that wonderful couscous!' or 'The night we decided to have a kid was amazing – we had candyfloss!' Personally, I think I potentially get it the wrong way round. The food is always the overriding memory. Take this conversation I had recently with my wife.

> *Me*: 'Do you remember when we were on holiday in Japan, and we had that fantastic pork katsu sandwich in the park?'
> *Charlie*: 'You mean the day you proposed to me?'
> *Me*: 'Yes, that happened too, I guess. But that sandwich!'

As you can probably tell, being in a relationship with someone who is food obsessed can be tricky, especially if you are not that way inclined. Dragged from restaurant to restaurant, constantly having to deal with waffle about ingredients and flavour profiles. At least, though, it will be the funniest reason to leave someone ever. I'd take that. While other people deal with infidelity and toxic partners, my wife will tell tales of how she finally had to get out because her husband spent an hour debating the merits of different types of capers. And when I am on my own, I can finally be sure that nobody will be ordering the same as me.

9

MARTINIS FOR ONE

I am approaching this chapter with caution. For many of you, the idea of drinking alone may be a red flag. The first sign of a problem that needs addressing. Drinking, we are told, should be done as a social activity with friends or colleagues and should not be part of our solitary lives. To an extent, I agree. Alcohol is a wonderful thing in company, a social lubricant that can lift an evening and help create wonderful moments. Memories of a rosé we drank on holiday, Christmas beers with the family, Prosecco at a birthday. Booze can merely be the background to more wholesome and soul-nourishing chapters in life. As soon as it becomes the focus of your stories, people start to become concerned for you. If you start bringing up with people the time you drank an amazing Martini at home by yourself, it's difficult for them to relate to. Firstly, they weren't there, and secondly, you sound like a raging addict.

There is something to be said, though, for solo drinking. You have to pick the type of drink very carefully, otherwise

it becomes bleak very quickly. The image of someone popping a bottle of champagne on their own is not a happy
one. It's a drink associated with landmark days, achievement and victory. None of these things should really be
celebrated by yourself at home. It's perfectly possible to
have a sense of achievement or victory alone, of course,
but marking this with a bottle of bubbly suggests an
unspoken darkness. Save the champagne. I can't imagine a
sadder sound than the pop of a cork in an empty house.
What is this person toasting? It's the sort of thing a rich
murderer might do after they've successfully offed their
spouse in an episode of *Columbo*. It's how they would
eventually be caught. 'Just one more thing before I leave
you to the funeral planning . . . I noticed there's half a
bottle of Moët on the sideboard. It's still fizzing, which
means you must've opened it after discovering your wife at
the bottom of the stairs. In the mood to celebrate, were we?'

It's the same with cocktails. This is more to do with the
process of making them. There are so many steps, so many
opportunities for you to realize that this is not the time for
mixing multiple ingredients for a drink you are simply
going to drain in front of *Coronation Street*. Chances are
there are people out there going all out for solo cocktails.
I'm talking umbrellas and sparklers. But such things should
only ever be added by someone who does not go on to
drink that drink. I can't imagine a much starker image than
someone lighting a sparkler, putting it in a drink, and then
having to blow out that sparkler and dispose of it safely, all
without saying a word to anyone else. That's the sort of

thing that should be on a public information poster about loneliness. Imagine a photo of a sad-looking old person. Now imagine that old person with a piña colada. Worse somehow, isn't it?

At home alone, the rule for drinks is no more than two ingredients. Any more than that and you have to be a barman who is practising. This is not to say that you shouldn't make cocktails at home, but they must be enjoyed with other people. I went through that phase. All my equipment sits in my living room – testament to another hobby I've abandoned. My house is a graveyard to lost hobbies. Between me and my wife, we could start an Etsy store for activity paraphernalia, much of which we could legitimately sell as brand new. If we cleared away my cocktail equipment, chin-up bar, kettlebells and comic books, and her pottery clay, crochet set and adult colouring books, we could have space for a child.

The cocktails were very much my thing for a while. I couldn't help but be impressed by those cool mixologists. The tossing and throwing of the shakers and the incorporation of weird ingredients no one's ever heard of was just so *sexy*. There are some things though, as I found out, that should be left to other people and never attempted at home. The first time I tried to throw a shaker in the air, I obviously dropped it and covered the kitchen in so much sticky liquid that it was like I was back in student halls. Eventually, I added so much ice to my shaking tin that the sudden change in temperature fused the lid to the cup and no amount of bashing and running it under a hot tap would free it. Having to dispose of a cocktail shaker full of old Espresso Martini was not exactly the *sexy* experience I had hoped for.

For drinking alone, you have to choose a certain kind of drink. Before that, you have to open yourself up to the fact that even doing it in the first place brings with it a certain level of bleakness. Then, if you want to proceed, you have to pick your poison. This must be connected with that bleakness. You need to select a brooding drink. Embrace the darkness. Red wine. Whisky. Brandy. Under no circumstances must you pick any clear spirits, white wine or anything fizzy. These are party drinks, designed for company. Imagine having a tequila at home alone? That, my friends, is the true meaning of Suicide Tequilas, in that it's tequila and if anyone finds you drinking it alone they'll assume you are about to kill yourself. You may as well have a solo Flimbo Limbo.

The benefit of the dark drinks is that they allow you to transport yourself to a different world. In this world, you are still alone drinking, but you have a reason. Red wine? Why, you are a poet. You are whiling away the wee hours in Regency France, contemplating the futility of existence and unrequited love. Of course you're drinking alone – your art demands it! Have a whisky alone and you are a grizzled Chicago cop, puzzling over the intricacies of a spate of murders on your patch. You need a whisky. You've seen so much. Plus your wife is dead. (Their wives are always dead.) Why not pour yourself a big brandy and imagine you are an ageing aristocrat, sitting up late by the fire and considering which of your children to cut out of the will? There are so many options. You can make solo drinking fun, but you have to make the right choices. It completely relies on your own imagination. Any outside observation spoils it completely. Imagine if someone walked into your house and saw you drinking a brandy alone? They wouldn't see the plotting aristocrat by the fire, they would see you, alone, drinking booze and pretending to warm yourself by a fire that doesn't exist. Worse still, you've put on one of those videos of a fireplace on YouTube. No, you need to be alone.

Drinking alone in a pub is a different matter. Solo drinking at home works because there are no prying eyes judging you. As soon as that precious bubble is popped, it becomes another experience. I do not have the confidence to drink alone in a pub where nobody knows me. I applaud those who do but I don't think I will ever be able to do it. When I used to nip into the pub where I worked, I had people I could chat to. I could at least pretend it was a social endeavour. There are some people who can go into a pub, order a drink and sit there reading a book or the paper and are totally fine with it. Or more astonishingly, sit there in complete silence with no added activity. These are the strongest people on the planet and should be studied by science. The joy of home solo drinking is you can imagine what you look like to others. You can conjure images of yourself as a sophisticated gourmand, considering the state of the world, because there is nobody else there to set you straight. In a pub you are surrounded by snitches. Any time I have attempted to have a pint alone to kill time, I couldn't hack it. I was anxious the whole time that everyone else in the pub was looking at me and discussing what my dark back-story was.

I know this because this is what I do to other people. It's actually one of my favourite hobbies. There's nothing more pleasurable than observing strangers and imagining their entire lives and what led them to this point, based on no evidence whatsoever other than what you see in front of you. The more outlandish and specific, the better. This game works well anywhere you might see someone alone. Public transport is a good option, but most of the time there is too sensible a reason for people to be alone on trains or buses. They are travelling somewhere. It's normal to be alone on public transport. Logic clouds the fun of imagin-ing what they might be doing. It works much better as a game in pubs and restaurants, traditionally places you would be with other people. When I was working in the pub, my main regret was that there wasn't time to play this game. And most of the solo-drinking regulars, to be fair to them, made it very clear why they were alone via their per-sonalities. There was very little room for imagination. One particular man would come in every day. You knew when he was about to arrive because you could smell him from the other side of the door. It was very clear why he was on his own.

Solo non-alcoholic drinking, of course, is always an option, and a less sad-looking one, too. As I hope you'll recall me suggesting a few chapters ago, not drinking at all is far more preferable to stopping at one drink. Or, as my mum used to suggest, interspersing alcoholic drinks with soft drinks. This was what she used to gently nudge me towards in my early years of drinking. Every two pints, she would say, why not have a Diet Coke? This is such a mum thing to say. I do understand what she was trying to do, and I appreciate it. The drinking culture at my school was fairly out of control, and this was her polite way of trying to calm me down. There was absolutely no way I was going to do it though. The nights out with my school friends, and then my uni friends, were such that having a softie was one of the worst social faux pas you could make. Everyone there was trying to get as drunk as possible, as quickly as possible. Coming back from the bar with a DC halfway through a session would be tantamount to whipping your trousers and pants down and plopping your genitals on to the table. That's a bad example, come to think of it. If someone came back from the bar and slapped their gennies out they would be welcomed like a hero returning from war. I went to public school, in case you hadn't worked it out.

In those days there was absolutely no excuse for not getting hammered. The drinking escalated from the early teens cans-on-the-common years, so by the time we reached an age when we could gain access to a pub, things were already off the rails. That age, by the way, was not eighteen. We weren't going to wait until then before we went to the pub. At around fifteen began the mission of us intrepid explorers, scouring south-west London for pubs that would gladly serve us even though the majority of us looked well under age. I don't know what things are like now, but we found plenty of establishments that were willing to flout the law and let large groups of teenagers drink illegally. If these places were still open, I would think twice about naming them, lest anyone under eighteen reading this book saw it as a list of recommendations. They have, to my knowledge, all been closed down (I can't even begin to think why). So, here goes. The Railway Inn (yes, a pub opposite a station), the King of Denmark and the Litten Tree. The King of Denmark was down the road from our school and would let us drink in there with our uniforms on. It felt like something from Victorian times, when ale was considered basic hydration and kids would drink it to strengthen their constitutions (no research here). The fact that you could smoke in pubs back then really helped the atmosphere, making every trip to the pub feel like a clandestine trip to a criminal den.

The fact that people used to be able to smoke indoors really is insane when you recall it now. Every trip out would always end with your clothes and hair absolutely reeking, regardless of whether you smoked or not. You could even smoke in restaurants. The one place where your senses of taste and smell should really be on top form and people were legally allowed to desecrate it. Yes, I suppose places did employ the genius idea of 'smoking areas'. There may be people reading this who aren't old enough to remember this stroke of innovation. Let me explain it to you. You'd walk into a restaurant and the greeter would offer you 'smoking or non-smoking?' You might think, 'Oh, I'll pick non-smoking – there's no way I want my burger and chips to be ruined by the smell of cigarettes.' Well, bad luck. Because the smoking area was simply a few randomly assigned tables separated from the rest of the room by NOTHING. No barriers, no glass enclosure, no wall. Just air. If there's one thing that we know smoke and smell love to waft on, it's air. That's what it travels through. Every trip to a restaurant non-smoking section was a trip to the smoking area. The mad thing is, we accepted it! Even when people finally cottoned on to the deadly danger of passive smoking, we put up with it. We found out that something could kill us and we happily sat across the room as it edged closer and closer towards us. If someone said that you could go in a room for a meal but there was an armed serial killer in there, would you do it? What if the waitress kindly offered you a seat in the non-killer section? You'd assume that maybe the murderer was behind bars perhaps, or in a Hannibal-style Perspex cell. Well, no. As you tuck into your starter, he is going to edge closer and closer to you until he is within stabbing distance. Madness. That's what we were doing. Ignoring the threat and ploughing on regardless. Thank God the government have learnt their lesson and would never again mishandle an airborne toxin.

Drinking at my school was a toxic culture, and at the time, I'm ashamed to say, I revelled in it. As we've already established, I am a weak sheep. If you didn't drink, and drink heavily, you weren't in the gang. So there was no opportunity to take my mother's advice for fear of ridicule. It wasn't just our school, of course. We were representative of British drinking as a whole, which was out of control at the time but is still tied distinctly to an ancient idea of masculinity and social ritual. Think about what we call non-alcoholic drinks – 'soft' drinks. This is specifically designed to sound weak. If you order anything that doesn't get you drunk, you are 'soft'. Alcoholic drinks, even more worryingly, aren't even regularly called 'hard' drinks. They are just called 'drinks'. It's like they're the only option, or at least the default. If someone asks you to go out for a drink, we assume that alcohol will be involved. Even now, at a time of life when I feel like I have more agency, if someone suggests we go for a drink and I'm off alcohol, I will feel the need to specify this to them. 'Just so you know, I'm only going to have soft drinks.' As if my sober personality isn't enough to sustain a night out and they might want to cancel. To be fair, it isn't, and they do.

The language of 'soft' drinks is well established. If my friends at the time had had a chance to rename them, they would've gone further. Anyone who was caught with a non-alcoholic drink would've been accused of having a 'coward liquid' or 'pussy juice'. (That last one probably needs more work.)

Our dogged attitude to drinking stretched way beyond the understanding that everyone would participate in consuming copious amounts of alcohol. The phrase 'eating's cheating' was often uttered. Those of you who come from similar boozy backgrounds may be familiar with this jolly little maxim. It's normally shouted at anyone who dares to suggest that you go for dinner before or during a binge-drinking session. Let's be clear about this: that is absolutely the most sensible thing to do. It was completely illogical that we decided that eating food was cheating, not to mention unhealthy. For a start, our self-worth was tied to how much we could drink in a single sitting, and eating would've meant we could drink more. Also, 'cheating'? I wasn't aware that the first time I had a sip of alcohol I had entered into a game with rules. I thought I was growing up, taking another step into adulthood and independent thought. No, apparently not. We were continuing childish behaviours, just with much higher stakes.

The idea behind 'eating's cheating', as far as I'm aware, was this. If we didn't line our stomachs, we would get much drunker much faster, and in turn feel much sicker. This was, I assume, a good thing. Nobody was concerned with the evening being nice throughout. Everything was focused on that first two hours and be damned if we all ended up vomiting or feeling terrible the next day. The phrase was shouted at people with the sort of fervour that is normally reserved for a sportsman caught in a doping scandal. It was as if we were a drinking team at the International Booze World Cup and if we were caught eating, the governing body would disqualify us.

Well, I have an admission to make to any of my old drinking buddies who may be reading this. I cheated. All the time. Before every night out we had, I ate a full meal. I believed in lining my stomach. Not, as you did, with eating *after* drinking and pointlessly dumping the lining on top of all the damage you'd already done. My mum would cook me a big hearty dinner, I would have one or two (or three) helpings, and then I'd meet you in the pub. When you all had kebabs and pizzas afterwards, yes, I ate those as well. Not because I was hungry, but because I love kebabs and pizzas. I know at the time I joined in with the cries of 'eating's cheating', but that's because I wanted to fit in. Eating is not cheating. Dinner is a winner. And you know what else? I cheat even more now. Sometimes, my favourite nights out are when I go for dinner and that is the whole night. I'll drink, but with food, and it makes me feel much nicer. If I do go out afterwards and I feel like I'm getting too drunk, guess what? Every couple of alcoholic drinks I'll have a soft drink instead. It took me a while to listen to my mum, but here we are. A thirty-seven-year-old mummy's boy who hasn't vomited from alcohol since 2017 and is proud of it.

Because for me then, as is the case now, my love of food far outweighed my love of booze. I enjoy alcohol, sure, but if it was banned tomorrow, I would not frequent a speakeasy or protest in the streets. If the government tries that with cheese, though, I will burn this fucking country to the ground.

10

TEETHMARKS IN THE CHEESE

If the film *Trainspotting* was about cheese and not heroin, I would find it much more relatable. I'm not sure that when Irvine Welsh first wrote the novel relatability was necessarily what he was aiming at to be fair to the guy, but my point stands. I would totally understand the exploits of Renton, Spud, Sick Boy and Begbie if they were all desperately running around Scotland chasing the creamy and salty high that only a massive wedge of cheese can bring. Hallucinating a baby on the ceiling? No, thanks! It's a Babybel on the ceiling for me every time, please and thank you. I've not tried heroin (yet), but I don't see how it could be comparable to a good Stilton or a mature Comté. I don't *need* to try brown, I have yellow and blue. Why have crack when I have crackers?

What I'm saying is, I love cheese. Always have, always will. Until the day I die. I would like to be buried in a coffin that looks like a wedge of Cheddar – which would be hugely ironic as cheese is almost certainly what will eventually kill me.

I don't have a distinct memory of the first time I ate cheese and fell in love with it. It's almost as if it's always been there. It wasn't the first food I had, I'm sure of that. I guess that was breast milk, but at least that is cheese-adjacent. As a baby, I probably thought to myself, 'Yes, this is nice, but it's not quite there yet. One day I'll have this experience again, but better. Someone will add cultures and rennet and I will be in heaven.' If I'd been a smart baby I would've reserved some of my stash and then, when my mum wasn't looking, secretly made tit mozzarella.

That sort of image doesn't even put me off cheese. I'm not actually sure what would put me off cheese. We often hear about these sushi parties where diners eat off a naked body. I like sushi, but I would draw the line at eating it at that party. I'd get a burger on the way home. Cheese off a naked person? No problem at all. I would eat a cube of Swiss out of any orifice that it happened to be presented on, or indeed in. In the past I've been dissuaded from foods that have gone mouldy or made me sick, but this isn't the case for cheese. Mouldy cheese is simply blue cheese. I love blue cheese. Also, cheese has made me sick on multiple occasions and it's never put me off.

My grandma used to make the most wonderful lasagne. The key to a good lasagne? Well, you could just flick forward to my special recipe, or I can tell you the answer now: more cheese than seems humane. Both my grandma's lasagne and the one I make now (see p. 232) are an insult to Italians. The amount of cheese packed in there is enough for me to risk detention at Rome airport. But you know what? I don't care. I laugh as I make it, imagining what a *nonna* from Bologna might say if she saw me building this terrifyingly cheesy Viennetta. But before my lasagne came my grandma's. I am standing on the shoulders of a giant and it would be disingenuous of me not to recognize that. I would eat helping after helping, continuing to eat against the advice of everyone around me. Even when everyone had cleared up and gone to bed, I would still be at the table, licking the dish clean like a big dirty lasagne dog. Of course, the meat sauce and the pasta were delicious and necessary. If my grandma had simply presented us with a bubbling pot of molten cheese everyone else would have baulked. Not me though. I would've appreciated the honesty of that. The pasta and meat are just vehicles for the cheese, a way of making the fact that we're eating four different varieties of cheese in one mouthful socially acceptable.

That's where I differ from a lot of people who claim to like cheese. They see it as a complement to other ingredients, as a backing singer to the band that is the meal. Not so here. That cheese is the star. It should go solo. It's only really the Swiss and the French who understand this and who have nearly nailed it with fondue. I say nearly, because they still dip bread in it. No need, guys! Grab a spoon and go bareback! That, to me, would be the perfect meal. I'm here to say that cheese does not need a vehicle. Cheese is perfectly capable of walking by itself – ideally right into my waiting mouth. Yes, a neat-cheese fondue would make me feel ill. But I would not care, and it would not divert me from my path. My grandma's lasagne, in the amounts I ate it, regularly made me sick. I will never forget the night I ate so much of it that I vomited off a bunk bed. That was the last time my cousin let me sleep on the top. I can't imagine the shock of waking up in the middle of the night, hearing an odd noise and then witnessing a cascade of puke pouring down from above. Nothing hit him, luckily, but there was so much of it that getting out of the bed to exit the room (as he obviously did immediately) was a trickier proposition than it should've been. Did that for one second make me want to eat less cheese? Did it hell. I'm sure for him it was a different story. That was probably the last time he went anywhere near the stuff, apart from in a recurring nightmare. As a child, I was once ill after I ate some baklava. I haven't eaten baklava since. But cheese is my beloved. Cheese until I die (of cheese)!

The variety is what really amazes me. 'Cheese' is such a narrow umbrella term and gives nowhere near enough credit to the breadth of the cheese world. It comes in all different shapes, sizes, flavours and colours. Someone saying they like cheese is like someone saying they like music. This tells us nothing. We need specifics! Hip hop? Death metal? Polka? Tell us more! You claim to like cheese, but what's your passion? Which one will you snaffle first? Do you favour the raw, uncompromising blast of a Stinking Bishop (the black metal of the cheese world) or, indeed, the smooth vibes of a soft goat's cheese (very much the cheese equivalent of lounge jazz)?

When I was a wee lad, I thought that Cheddar was the only cheese. This can be an issue in the UK sometimes.

Cheddar gets most of the press, and unless you're willing to dig deeper, you're never going to discover some of the underground hits. When I turned seven, the only food I demanded at my birthday was cheese and pineapple on sticks. There's a reason for Cheddar here, granted: it complements the pineapple well and is one of the best cheeses structurally to be stick-compatible. I love a Stilton, but as soon as a cube of that goes on a cocktail stick it is crumbling and leaving stinky residue all over the guests. There's only one type of party where guests should be leaving with stinky residue on them, and it's not a seven-year-old's birthday party. I don't even remember being particularly bothered about having a cake. I loved cake and still do, but it's never the highlight of an event for me. It normally comes out at a time when everybody has already eaten loads of other stuff, and it's annoying to cut up and distribute. As a spectacle, it's A+. I love the candles, I love the ritual of blowing them out and I love how fancy and colourful cakes can be. It's a bit showy though. Cake never lives up to what it looks like. Cheese doesn't need all that flash bang. It doesn't put on a show, it simply arrives and does its job. I remember saying all that to my mum when we were planning the party. 'Mum, cheese doesn't put on a show,' I said, 'it just turns up and does its job.' After we got back from the child psychologist, we planned the rest of the party.

I must've had cheese and pineapple on sticks at another party and that gave me the idea. I don't remember it, but that must've been the case. There's no way I invented cheese and pineapple on sticks when I was a child, is there? If I had, that's what this whole book would be about. I would be a child prodigy, cruelly robbed of the plaudits he deserved for inventing one of the finest party foods known to man. It would no doubt cover the day I came up with the concept, the birthday party in question, and then the tale of how I was robbed of my intellectual property by some evil child rival, hellbent on taking my idea. Then the endless court cases, of course, where I eventually prove that the idea was all mine, thanks to an Etch-a-Sketch on which I had done the initial blueprints. Sort of like *The Social Network* but with an invention that has done nothing but good for the world. In truth, I think cheese and pineapple on sticks is a classic party food that started in the 1970s. Which makes the fact that I was obsessed with it as a young child even more ridiculous. All the rest of my peers were sweet crazy, jonesing for the next sugar hit from any chocolate or ice cream they could find, while I was swanning around with a handful of used cocktail sticks like a character from *Abigail's Party*.

Also, if I had invented it I wouldn't have added the pineapple. I return to my point about cheese vehicles. I think I was probably ashamed at the time to ask for just cheese on sticks, but that's what I would've wanted. Pure, unadulterated cheese straight into my system, unsullied by this pineapple-cutting agent. If you want pineapple, have pineapple. If you want cheese, let it do its thing. There's a high chance that at this party I didn't even speak to any of my friends, I just hung out by the snacks, carefully removing the pineapple. I don't remember much about that party other than the P&C on sticks, apart from the fact I was dressed as a cowboy even though it definitely wasn't a fancy-dress event. I wouldn't have cared though. I had a holster full of cheese and I was quick on the draw. No pineapple though – my town wasn't big enough for the both of them.

After that point, my adoration of cheese was truly cemented. If there was cheese in the fridge, I was eating it. One morning my mum called me downstairs. I knew I was about to be told off because she called me Edward. This was and is only reserved for a telling-off. When I was eleven or twelve, I had made the decision to be known as Ed. This is a big life moment for any child. I was leaving life as Edward behind me. Most names work in full or shortened, but the name Edward needs to be clipped as soon as possible. You do not want to be an adult Edward. You can imagine that guy. He takes himself very seriously, he sneers when he doesn't agree with you, and he is no stranger to a cravat. Adult Edwards shouldn't exist. They should be relegated to being villains in Victorian novels. If you are an adult Edward reading this, I am not sorry. You are not a fun person and you need to lighten up. Even the adult Jonathans and Anthonys are more of a laugh than you. I would implore any potential parents not to name their child Edward. Go with Ed, Eddy, Eddie or Ted. You are going to have a fun kid! Eds and Eddies are a laugh! Edwards are not a laugh. Edwards own napkin rings.

It pains me every day that I have to be Edward on official documents. Whenever I present my passport to an official when I'm travelling, I swear I see their heart sink when they see what my full name is. They probably think twice about letting me into their country. I think they should stand by it. 'I'm sorry, sir, we can't possibly let in an Edward. We here in Argentina try to have more of a relaxed vibe, and just from reading your name I can tell you're a stuffy twat who's probably packed teabags in his suitcase. DENIED.' The truth of the matter is, I'm not even that happy with Ed. I always wished I was called Rick, after Rik Ricicle from the Ricicles box. Now, that guy was cool. All Ricks are cool, but Rik Ricicle was an astronaut AND had his own cereal. You can't ask for much more than that. But I had to stick with the hand I'd been dealt, albeit after discarding a few of the cards. Ed it was, and Ed it remains. Edward is for bank statements and when my mum tells me off.

On this occasion, it wasn't a big telling-off. It was more of a baffled and curt enquiry. She wanted to know why there were teethmarks in the block of Cheddar. That's a tricky one to lie about. Anything you do to attempt to prove your innocence would be immediately rejected in a court of law. There's clear dental evidence. I was busted. I considered saying that a fox must've slipped in through the cat flap, but there were more holes in that plan than in a slice of Leerdammer. The teeth that had taken the chunk clearly weren't those of a fox. I would've had to keep adding to my story and said that the fox must've stolen some false teeth from the old lady next door, but by that point in a lie you're barely keeping your head above water. As they always say in law school, 'If a witness says they saw a fox with false teeth then you know you've got them backed into a corner.' I would also have had to explain why a fox with falsies would come into our house via the cat flap, manage to open a fridge door, disturb nothing apart from the cheese, and then politely leave again after shutting the fridge. Also, we didn't have a cat flap. As we've learnt from most detective shows, sometimes the simplest explanation is the right one.

As was the case here. The accused (me, Ed Gamble) had felt peckish, walked to the fridge and simply taken a bite out of the corner of the Cheddar block like a big mouse. It wouldn't have taken Poirot to figure it out, and Anne Gamble had me bang to rights. There was a lot of 'Why didn't you use a knife and a plate?' and 'How am I supposed to eat this cheese now?' flying about, and a bigger man might've held his hands up and admitted that, yes, these were valid complaints. As we've established, I was a fairly big man, because of all the cheese I ate. I was also the only man in the house because my parents were separated, but that's by the by. Still, I wasn't about to back down to my mother's nit-picking.

The fact is, I don't agree that you *need* a plate and a knife to enjoy cheese. Cheese is a hand food, like an apple or a hot dog. If you saw someone tucking into an apple with a knife and fork on a plate, you would rightly assume that they were billy bonkers. Cheese is the same. Cutlery as a concept has oppressed us for far too long in Western society and it's time we realized that we should be doing a lot more with the hands that God gave us. (I don't actually believe in God until it comes to arguing about cheese. It helps my case, and I genuinely can't conceive that cheese was created by anything other than a divine being.)

Cheese is designed for the hand. Take the example of a block of Cheddar. Imagine holding it in your hand. It's the ideal size, and a satisfying weight. It's as close as you can get to intelligent design. You're telling me that you don't want to just take a bite? I suppose you would say you need to slice or grate it if you wanted cheese on toast. Nope. Bite off chunks and spit them on to the bread. Much quicker, and you get your mouth excited for the cheese to come. Even better, stop being so weak and stop having cheese on toast. Eat the cheese, and if you really want some toast, have that afterwards. It all ends up in your stomach together anyway. 'Surely you don't eat pre-grated cheese with your hands, Ed?' Well, yes, I do. I pinch that stuff up and put it in my mouth like it's chewing tobacco and I'm a grandad cowboy sitting on a stoop.

Many of you sheeple will be claiming that the knife is important for slicing and portioning among many people. To you I say, wake up! Take a bite of the cheese and if someone else wants some, pass it round. This is much more convenient and has the added bonus of bringing people together. It's a communal cheese experience. The peace pipe of the dairy world. Imagine the scene at dinner. Conversation has been stilted all night, I bet. You know why? Because you have all been eating from separate plates, using your stupid little cutlery. Then at the end of the evening, some forward-thinking bright spark brings in a block of cheese. 'How are we going to eat that?' your weak and tiny voice says. You can't wrap your puny mind around what is about to happen. Then, this handsome and brilliant genius takes a chomp from the cheese. Your brain is blown out of the top of your thick skull. 'What is this guy *doing*?!' you think. 'This goes against everything we've ever been taught! This man is sexy, sure, but is he also one of the great minds of our time?! It seems so!' Then the man (imagine it's me if that's easier) passes the block to the person sitting next to him and encourages them to take a bite. They do. The man urges them to pass it to the next person. Now you're getting the hang of it! Before long, everyone is talking. Not the awkward small talk that characterized the start of the evening, but really *talking*.

Anyway, when I said this to my mum she didn't seem to care. She just muttered something about it being disgusting.

Cheese on sticks and nibbles from the fridge were an inevitable gateway to the big leagues. The cheeseboard. I love a cheeseboard. It's the cheese lover's nirvana. It's an opportunity to eat as many different kinds of my favourite thing and to travel the world, all on one single board. As a committed follower of the concept, I am always eager to spread the word of my savoury saviour to the masses. And what do a lot of people like? Football. If we can push the joy of the cheeseboard to football fans, I think we can make this country a better place. Imagine the scenes at the grounds! Grey burgers and cones of wet chips replaced with planks of the finest cheeses. I should say that I don't know anything about football. But if there was cheese available at the games? Sign me up. This is my attempt to sell the idea to footy fans in a language they understand.

IF A CHEESEBOARD WAS A FOOTBALL TEAM (BY A MAN WITH NO KNOWLEDGE OF FOOTBALL)

Goalkeeper: **Mature Cheddar**

The perfect choice to tend to the goal. Strong, solid and reliable, mature Cheddar is always there for you. Even if all your other players (cheeses) are sent off (can this happen in football?), I feel confident that mature Cheddar will do its job. When I say mature, I mean really mature. A cheese that has seen a lot and learnt from every game. The sort with those crystals in. A gritty and resilient player that is a must for any cheeseboard team sheet.

Defenders: **Manchego, Comté, Cornish Yarg, Double Gloucester**

An impenetrable backline of hard and semi-hard cheeses. You don't want to mess with these lads. There is some international flair on display with Manchego and Comté, but Yarg and DG balance this out with some good old-fashioned British resilience. They get on well with the goalie and each other, and it's unlikely they'll lose their place on this team any time soon.

Central Midfielders: **Goat's Cheese, Truffle Brie**

Both of these players have a soft and creamy style of play that is irresistible. Goat's Cheese is deceptively subtle but has a sharp kick that can sneak up on the opposition if they underestimate it. Truffle Brie is an expensive signing, but worth every penny. He needs a bit of time on the field before he really comes into his own, but when he does, he is a marvel.

Wingers: **Gruyère, Wensleydale**
These guys lull the opposition into a false sense of security. Everyone assumes that Gruyère's game is full of holes and that Wensleydale will crumble at the first touch. Underestimate them at your peril. They'll be past you before you know it. Don't make the mistake of playing Cranberry Wensleydale. He is a shade of the player his older brother is and belongs in the lower leagues (the bin).

Strikers: **Stilton, Roquefort**
Now we're talking. The blue power duo that cannot be stopped. Every time you play them, they score. The opposition are scared of their pungency and strength, but behind that they are complex, undeniable and powerful. They've never let the side down.

Subs bench: **Grapes, Chutney, Crackers, Quince**
Rarely played and, if I'm honest, useless. The team is perfect. Mainly there for the aesthetics and in case of extra time.

THE PITCH

The best option for me is to serve the cheese on an actual board, by the way (barring the hitherto unexplored and revolutionary idea of serving the cheeses on another huge slice of cheese. Watch this space, I'm working on it.) The board is the most rustic and pleasing option.

I've talked a lot about the transportive nature of food and

drink, their ability to take you to another place, another body even. This is what the board does to me. A simple piece of wood makes me feel like I am a hard-working farmer, probably with something like corn or whatever those yellow plants are that you see by the side of the M4. Not in now times though – that's no fun. If you're going to have fun with your imagination, you are severely limiting your options if you stay in the present. A simple mouthful can help you travel through time, so don't waste it! The cheeseboard fantasy is a journey into the past. It would be difficult to imagine you're in the future while eating cheese. Dairy will no longer be available in a hundred years' time, so best save the future visions for something like those sachets of astronaut food or drinking wine from a can.

No, when I am eating cheese from a plank I am a farmer in the past. I'm not sure when exactly, but there are no electric lights. That's probably a good thing, because I look *rough*. My hands are red raw from steering my horse-drawn plough (those horses are strong, and they bite) and my cheeks are blotchy from working in the icy cold all day. I have a wife in this fantasy, by the way, as I do in real life. Bad news for my actual wife, though: it's not her. No, it's a stout lady who is the local nurse, also run off her feet looking after lepers, etc. It's been a rough year for the harvest and the village (Derby?), so food is hard to come by. But each night we lovingly prepare a simple meal of different cheeses, all hand-made from milk from the local cows, goats and women (I don't know what people did in the past). Paired with a simple hunk of bread, we tear into them voraciously, just for a moment forgetting that we had to sell all of our children to raise money to pay for their tuition. Also, we crack open a bottle of wine that I've made by treading grapes with my awful feet. The cheeses are presented on a board. Not on a plate, not on a glass stand, and in the name of all that is holy not on a slate. I do not want my cheese to be brought to me on a slate, EVER. Slates are for roofs and, in very exceptional circumstances, for local children to throw at ducks after they fall off the roofs.

THE EXILES

Yes, I love cheeseboards. It's not something I fake to annoy James Acaster on *Off Menu*. They are the best bit of Christmas. If my family banned me from seeing them on Christmas Day, my tree caught fire and my television broke, I would not care. As long as I had my cheeseboard. I would warm myself by the tree fire and declare it the best Christmas ever, as I do every year when I have my first bite of cheese.

There is, however – and I can't believe I'm saying this – an issue with cheeseboards. Cheeseboards – and this really does pain me to say – are stuck in their ways. They are from the old school. Not racist per se, but I wouldn't be surprised if the guy who invented them was cancelled on Twitter at some point. I've thought for hours now for a good pun-based name on who invented cheeseboards. The closest I've come is the celebrity cyclist Chris Boardman, if you change his name slightly to Cheese Board-man. I'll just leave it. For God knows how long, there have been certain cheeses that have simply not been allowed on the board. The drawbridge has been pulled up. There's been a glass ceiling for cheese. No matter how popular these cheeses get, they have never been allowed on the board.

Well, this is their time. Writing this book, as I see it, has given me a lot of power. The food industry will be looking to me to make important decisions. I guess I've become somewhat of an icon who can now change things up and use my platform for good. So, here are the three cheeses I am OFFICIALLY adding to the standard cheeseboard line-up.

Feta

What does feta have to do to get a look in? For over a decade now, it has proved itself. It goes with *everything*. It is clearly the most versatile of all the cheeses. Salad, omelettes, meat, roasted veg, pasta – hell, you can even just bake it and eat it straight. Yes, it's the saltiest of all the cheeses. Maybe that's why. All the other cheeses are scared of it. It's an all-rounder, and while they swan around claiming to be salty, here comes feta to kick the living shit out of them. It would dominate, and that's why people are terrified.

Well, I say, have a bit of backbone. Don't be afraid of feta's prowess. If the other cheeses can't stand up to it, maybe you shouldn't be blaming feta, and instead get the other cheeses to up their game a little. Feta is one of my go-to-straight-out-of-the-fridge cheeses. It's a meal in itself. Just a few cubes of that and I'm ready for my day (after two pints of water to quench my thirst). I hereby add feta to the traditional cheeseboard.

Halloumi

Do people have issues with the Greeks or something? The first time I remember tasting halloumi was on holiday as a child in Cyprus, in a beachside taverna. I'd been swimming all day (well, plopping around in the sea like a pale seal) and was starving. I had grilled halloumi and chips. It was, and is, in the top five meals I have ever had in my life. I had it every day of the holiday after that. It was only our pre-booked return flight to the UK (and the fact that I was a child) that meant I did not stay and am not still there now eating it again and again until I die a leathery old expat.

There's just something so magical about halloumi. It's not like any other cheese. It's like it was beamed down from an alien planet as a gift from a higher species. It's rubbery, salty and squeaky – none of which should work for food. A squeaky food? There's no way that should be delicious. Squeaks are for kittens and haunted doors, not dinner. But it works. It's not an inviting prospect when you buy it either. It comes in a plastic packet surrounded by a mystery liquid (lube?) and slops out on to a chopping board like a worrying emission. When you introduce that bad boy to heat, however, it's all like, 'Hey, heat, I'm halloumi, nice to meet you! I think you and I are going to get on very well indeed.' And get on they do. The best of pals. A grill, a BBQ, a pan – it doesn't matter what sort of heat you apply, the halloumi transforms into something your mouth simply isn't prepared for.

And God knows it's worked hard enough! Halloumi is mainstream. It's on the menu at Nando's. People put it in burgers, they make fries out of it. But can it infiltrate the elusive boys' club of the cheeseboard? No, it can't. Until now. I hereby add halloumi to the official cheeseboard line-up.

Cheese string

This is perhaps going to be the most controversial addition. But sometimes, change is hard to swallow. And sometimes, so is a cheese string. You're probably feeling uncomfortable now, aren't you? A weird feeling in the pit of your stomach? Well, you know what that feeling is called? Progress. It's called progress.

When they first came out, cheese strings changed the game. A simple yellow stick that looked like it had nothing going for it. Then you teased the side, and oh, the beauty! They fall and pull apart like a head of healthy blond hair for what seems like hours. Something that appears as if it won't last two seconds transforms into an entire meal's worth of dairy (?) magic.

When I first encountered the cheese string, I knew things would never be the same again. I eagerly awaited the inevitable follow-ups. Stilton String, Brie String, Dairylea String. Maybe they would branch out into other areas? They had the technology to stringify, so why stop at cheese? Yoghurt String, Beef String, Crisps String! The world was their oyster (which would also make a fabulous string). But they stopped. Cheese strings disappeared. Was this simply a case of the craze dying down? Or a conspiracy that went right to the top of the dairy industry, to Cheese Boardman himself?

I know what I think – but what about you? Will you continue to believe those in power, or will you join me and take the red pill (string)? I say no more! Bring back the cheese string! Yes, it may challenge the norm. Yes, it may taste absolutely horrible. But it's so fun to play with! I hereby add cheese strings to the traditional cheeseboard.

Yes, cheese is my life. In recent years, however, I've had to relegate it to more of a background role. When I made the decision to lose weight, I hung on to cheese as long as I could. I didn't want to believe that eating piles and piles of the stuff on a daily basis couldn't be part of my daily routine. I was an addict in denial. If there had indeed been a cheese angle to *Trainspotting*, I would undoubtedly have turned in the most convincing audition. Every other character would still be addicted to heroin, but I would've been the lone role that was in a cheese hole. My character name would've been Cheddar, of course, and I would've been best mates with Spud (there's no better combo). Because this addiction was very hard to shake. I was trying to make every aspect of my life healthier, but I just couldn't allow myself to realize that dropping my consistent cheese intake might be helpful to my aim. I was wearing cheese blinkers.

Please don't misinterpret me – I am not telling anyone how to eat or live their lives. Indulge in what you like. This is not a book that is promoting dieting (as you may have established from reading it). Bearing that in mind though, you must understand quite how much cheese I was eating. I would put it on *everything*. Every meal of the day would involve cheese. Because – and I still stand by this – cheese goes on everything. Back then, a typical daily menu might be like this:

Breakfast: *a cheese and ham omelette, with the cheese to ham ratio so biased in cheese's favour that you could barely taste the ham. It was pointless even calling it ham – all it was doing was providing colour. You were better off calling it 'cheese and pink omelette'. Even 'omelette' was stretching the definition. Yes, there was egg, but it really only served as an outer layer to keep the mountains of melted Cheddar in place. In essence, breakfast was a cheese and pink eggy pocket.*

Mid-morning snack: *a handful of those Marmite mini cheeses. These are as precious to me as diamonds, but I would never try and eat a diamond. I would, however, wear a Marmite cheese on my finger like a fancy ring. This snack would give me just the right amount of energy to carry out my daily tasks (thinking about cheese).*

Lunch: *Panini, pizza or anything else Italian that you could cram a lot of cheese into. The Italians are the ultimate cheese enablers. Every single Italian dish is either mainly cheese or is designed to have cheese sprinkled on top. Even their desserts invariably involve some sort of sweetened cheese. If I lived in Italy, I would be dead. Given that I would have died of cheese consumption and how much the Italians love cheese, I would probably now be canonized by the Vatican City. St Mozzarella*

Parmesanicus, the patron saint of dairy farmers. Has a nice ring to it, I think. If I was feeling restrained, I might have a tomato soup. This might sound like a real left turn in my daily habits. Don't fret though: I would dump in so much grated Cheddar that it would end up resembling a red fondue.

Dinner: *Back when I was still living with my mum, she would cook something. She was a tricksy chef and would often try and make things that seemingly had no relationship to cheese. No relationship to cheese if you had no ambition, that is. I could secretly put cheese on top of anything from any nation. If you haven't tried cheese on a roast dinner or a curry, you are living in a world without colour. Open your minds! If it's edible, cheese it!*

Pre-bed snack: *As previously revealed, I would bite a block of cheese.*

It was a real wrench to admit to myself that this much cheese couldn't be part of my more nutritious approach to life. I'd changed my diet a fair amount, the pizzas and burgers were gone for now, replaced with much more salad and veg, but the cheese had remained. There is only so much cheese you can add to a salad before it is no longer a salad. It's much less than you think. I was whacking in so much of the stuff that it looked like the leaves were accidental, as if they had dropped off a tree in a high breeze and contaminated the plate. For me, I had to establish a rule. No cheese in the house. I simply couldn't control myself around it, so it was removed from my shopping list completely.

This may seem drastic, and I am not recommending this as a plan of action for everyone. It's just that, if it's in the house, I will eat the whole lot immediately. I wouldn't even remember what had happened. I'd just black out and wake up next to empty packets. It was time for me and cheese to take a break. We'd been co-dependent for far too long, and it wasn't good for either of us. It was time for a new phase in my life.

My torrid affair with cheese may be over, but I'm happy to say that we now have a very modern open relationship. I have allowed my life to be filled with other foods, and I will frequently go days, even weeks, without satisfying my carnal lust for that manna from heaven. But every so often, when I really feel like the warm embrace of true love, I return to cheese. It's a life that works for us, and I don't care what the world thinks. Maybe one day we will be re-united perfectly and live in the same house on a permanent basis. But, for now, we are happier (largely) apart.

I I

TOFU STUNTMAN

There was a time when I forced myself to abstain completely from cheese. Believe it or not, at the age of thirty-two, for nine months of my life, I was vegan.

Ideally you would believe it, actually. If you didn't, that would make this bit pretty awkward. I thought we'd built up some trust so far in this book? The fact that you would consider abandoning that at this stage is quite distressing.

I can see why you might be sceptical, though. In the early chapters I extolled the virtues of consuming meat to such an extent that you might have mistaken me for some sort of libertarian American podcaster, obsessed with eating like our caveman forefathers did. In case you need it to be confirmed, I think that is insanity. To do something just because someone did it in prehistoric times is bananas – or as a caveman would say, 'those weird yellow things that don't scream when I club them'. I would go so far as to say that most things I do, I do them as little like a caveman as possible. What else should I be doing?

Wearing little fur knickers and using a pelican as a cement mixer? I'll stick to a varied diet, if you please. Cavemen didn't even have Soleros.

Although I may not have been a thick-skulled meat evangelist, the fact remains that I was eating it on a regular basis. Most days, if I'm honest. So, when I tell people that I was completely vegan for a period of my life, they are understandably shocked. 'You?!' they might say. 'But I once saw you eat a whole chicken, bones included, with your bare hands before washing them in pig blood!' This isn't wholly representative, although I definitely have bitten clean through a chicken bone now and again. Not through any misplaced meaty masculinity, I am just frequently simultaneously hungry and lazy.

Some readers may be shocked for a different reason. They may think I am still vegan. During my period of living the plant life, I made the horrible mistake of saying I was vegan on the BBC2 panel show *Mock the Week*. I had promised myself that I wouldn't be public about my decision and certainly not within the first year. Shamefully, the comedian in me took over, I saw an opportunity for a joke about it, and I proclaimed on a widely watched national television show that I was vegan. Even worse than that, it was in response to Tom Allen, who had made the observation that all vegans talk about is being vegan. So, naturally, I mentioned I was vegan at every given opportunity throughout the whole taping. Big mistake. If this was TV in the old days, I might've got away with it. But these days, shows do not disappear. It went on to iPlayer, where it was watched by even more people, and, even worse, on to Dave, where it continues to be repeated thousands of times to this day. Dave is like a drunk gossipy family member who will not keep a secret and will bring it up at every event possible. Never say something you might regret if you think it might make it to Dave. You'll never hear the end of it. So, even now, if I mention eating meat, or eat meat publicly, I am guaranteed a raft of messages from people saying things like 'I thought you were vegan' and 'Doesn't look very vegan.' Thanks, Dave.

Given my affinity for eating flesh, then, why did I go vegan? This is a tricky question to answer. Most people begin a vegan lifestyle for ethical reasons, environmental reasons or health reasons. All of these things definitely concerned me (and still do). I like animals, I don't want to destroy the planet, and I don't want to have a heart attack. I suppose if I had to order these concerns, I would go with animals, planet, health. Health is at the bottom, because quite frankly if I die of a heart attack then I won't have to see the planet burn and the animals will have at least got their own back somehow. Each of these concerns definitely played on my mind when I decided to make the shift, but I'm not sure any of them was the overriding factor.

I think, shamefully, I just wanted a new challenge. Losing weight and running a marathon had proved that I had a potential for willpower that nobody had expected, least of all me. I wanted that feeling again – to feel like I had the capacity to shock and impress people. Yes, somehow, I found the only way to become vegan for selfish reasons. It's quite

an incredible feat if you think about it. Veganism is a move-
ment associated with kindness and selflessness, yet I
managed to turn it into a vanity project.

I quickly found out, though, that people are far less
wowed by veganism than they are by weight loss or running quite far. Most people were baffled or just downright
annoyed. Telling someone I was vegan would often elicit a
roll of the eyes or a 'Why?!' Even worse, I found myself
subjected to old-school vegan stereotypes – that they are
all smug hippies – and straight-up abuse. Yes, people who
say these kinds of things still exist and are often younger
than you might assume. They tell you that vegans love to
tell you that they are vegan, and that they love to feel super-
ior. This is not true of any vegan I know. They just get on
with it. They don't preach, they don't lecture. They're far
too busy looking for a leaf symbol on a menu. Annoyingly,
it was probably true of me when I was vegan. I did love telling people, mainly because I was expecting some kind of
pat on the back, or to be compared to Captain Planet. So,
if I helped with anything during my plant-based tenure, it
was to confirm untrue assumptions about vegans being
self-righteous. You're welcome.

The diet aspect I struggled with far less than I had
expected. In this day and age, I'm told it is way easier to be
vegan. Brands and restaurant chains have finally caught on
and realized that there is profit to be made from offering
plant-based options. In the before times, you hear about
the ordeals vegans had to go through when eating out. The
choices were either small independent cafés run by Hare

Krishnas, only having chips or eating a pine cone from nearby scrubland. Now, they can walk into a McDonald's or a Burger King and have their needs seen to. This must be a weird feeling, though, especially if you are vegan for ethical reasons. These companies may have started catering for vegans, but they are still slinging out meat left, right and centre. You may be doing something virtuous, but you are still plainly up to no good. It's like a crèche opening in Vatican City. On balance, it's probably a good thing that the options are there, despite it clearly being done for profit rather than anything more wholesome.

On the rare occasion I go to a fast-food restaurant now (drunk, or feeling sad), I will normally opt for the plant-based choice. This is because for me their normal fare is so far from tasting like meat anyway that the alternatives are almost exact carbon copies. Their carnivorous standards seem to rise little higher than someone mashing up a load of wet cardboard, slapping it on a grill and whispering 'meat' into the bun. The vegan burgers aren't much better taste-wise, but at least you can feel good about yourself while you chew through one.

I can see why new vegans might find vegan alternatives to meat helpful. It helps ease the transition away from their previous lifestyle. I do think, though, that science has started to take it too far. There is now a burger available that is completely plant-based but which 'bleeds' like meat. Nobody was asking for that. Even now that I have returned to Team Meat, I would say that things bleeding isn't high on my list of priorities. Yes, I like rare steak, but that is all based on taste, rather than the sight of the blood itself. I already feel guilty enough about my actions, and the reminder of the suffering I have helped inflict isn't a plus point. What next? A completely lab-created bacon that screams when you bite it? Vegan ice cream that has synthesized the taste of calf tears? I don't know why veganism thinks that it needs to try so hard. They have vegetables on their team. Vegetables are delicious. With aubergines in the world, we don't need a fake steak that leaches gore on to the plate. If science had its way, it would take the humble and tasty aubergine and give it a spleen.

Having said that, during my short-lived vegan tenure I did struggle psychologically with the absence of meat. Vegetables are delicious, yes, but I couldn't help but feel that something was missing, regardless of how much scrambled tofu I was eating. Scrambled tofu, for those of you not in the know, is supposedly the vegan alternative to scrambled eggs. It will regularly pop up on café menus listed on their vegan breakfast, proudly proclaiming itself as a worthy stand-in for its evil chicken-butt bredrin. It's actually a pretty good like-for-like swap, presuming you close your eyes, hold your nose and you've never eaten eggs before. Good vegan alternatives should be like good stuntmen. You should barely notice the switch and just be able to immerse yourself in the action. Replacing scrambled eggs with scrambled tofu is the equivalent of me doing a stunt for The Rock. The beautiful and tasty eggs are replaced by something white, wobbly and tasteless (a description that works for me as well as for tofu). This is not to say that I did not regularly make scrambled tofu. Once I had the hang of it, it was quite delicious. You can pack it with spices and seasoning, and on toast it is a real treat. That, to be fair, goes for everything. I truly believe I could exist in a cannibal society as long as there was sourdough and a Breville. The actual process of making scrambled tofu, I found, was not as fun as scrambling eggs. Cracking an egg is one of life's great pleasures, and I don't care how sad that makes me sound. It can be surprisingly tricky, but once you've established your style it's like a magic trick. Personally, I go for a sharp tap on a flat surface and then use both thumbs to exploit the weakness that the impact has created. I tried for many years to use the crack-on-the-side-of-the-pan method, but this led to egg spillage, shelly omelettes (my drag name) and stressful breakfasts. One day, I hope to find an even more flamboyant egg-cracking method – my own unique style perhaps. I want to be the egg-cookery version of the policeman who turns his gun sideways in films. Maybe a throw in the air followed by a smooth catch where I seamlessly pull the egg in half? Maybe I will put the egg in my mouth, spit out the yolk and white and swallow the shell? For now, though, I am happy to be a basic breakfast bitch and crack like everyone else. The point is, this joy is missing in scrambled tofu. You have to crumble the tofu into chunks. Equally tactile, sure, but by no means as satisfying. You can pretend to be an ogre crushing the innards of a pathetic human, of course, but that electrifying snap of an eggshell is lacking. There is no scrambling to speak of, just a wet squelch as you push soy-bean curd through your moist fingers. I would pile seasoning into my scrambled tofu. Turmeric, smoked paprika, dried chilli, white pepper – anything I could lay my hands on. Most recipes also call for something called 'nutritional yeast', which, given how often vegans use it, you would've thought they could've come up with a better name for. 'Nutritional yeast' sounds like a supplement that people are fighting over in a post-apocalyptic scenario and it looks just as unpleasant. Imagine dried fish-food flakes that smell faintly of old cheese. Now pop that in your dinner. It adds a tang to dishes, certainly, but you really have to muster the courage to use it and be confident that it's going to improve your dish. All this really gives me much more of an understanding of what vegans have to go through to uphold their principles. The end result of scrambled tofu is delicious, but if anyone tells you that it stands in successfully for scrambled eggs? They are a liar and you should have them arrested.

Far worse, however, are the plant-based cheese alternatives. Those are a hate crime. I'm surprised they are legally allowed even to align themselves with God's own food. Sure, often they will get round the lawyers by calling them names like 'cheeze' or 'ch33s3', but we all know what they're suggesting: that what is inside the packet is nothing like anything approaching the sheer joy of a dairy cheese. In reality, they should call it 'nut paste disappointment' or 'cow's revenge'. I tried them all when I was vegan, but nothing could match up. To most people, I'm sure that the feeling of doing something good for the planet outweighs the taste of actual cheese, but as you have already heard, I am not most people when it comes to cheese. I am a purist. My love of cheese is far too strong to be wavered by ethical concerns. Yes, this might make me a bad person. Send me to jail. As long as that jail has Stilton, I'll be fine.

The fact that I publicly proclaimed myself vegan made the climbdown feel even more embarrassing. I had failed at being vegan. It was only a pass-or-fail situation in my head, I think. This is the way I approach most things. I'm very binary. I'm an extremely competitive person and this very much extends to competing with myself. Because my attempts had collapsed, I saw myself as weak-willed. But what a delicious failure it was.

It all fell apart very quickly and easily on a trip to Japan in 2018. Charlie (who became my fiancée during the trip) had informed me that it's quite difficult to eat vegan in Japan. We'd already endured a trip to the Caribbean that was fairly arduous. Ideally, that is not a sentence I want repeated out of context. Finding vegan options was tricky; I am not proclaiming that I have a hard life because I went on a trip to Barbados. My entire vibe is already too posh and entitled for my liking, so the insinuation that I'm making a sob story out of a trip to the West Indies might be the end of any sympathy people have for me. The things that people thought counted as vegan while we were there were wide-ranging, a particular highlight being when a waiter asked if chicken was OK. So, as soon as I received the tip that Japan might be difficult, I immediately did extensive research to see if this was true and where I might be able to eat in order to maintain this new life of mine.

That's a lie. I did no research, took it at face value, and immediately threw all my principles in the bin in favour of sushi and grilled meat skewers.

It's very difficult to come back from something like that. I returned to the UK and had no intention of picking up where I had left off. I was a lapsed vegan, and that was something I would have to live with. I like to think that I eat less meat now, so maybe some good has come out of it. I learnt to love tofu and can now see the true value of meals that have no meat. I used to think it didn't count unless it had meat in it. Now, I will happily eat vegetables and only vegetables without itching for a bit of animal. Although I usually ruin it by popping some cheese on the top.

So, please, take this chapter as my official announcement that I am no longer vegan. Spread it far and wide. Please stop messaging me about being vegan. I struggle enough with my decision without being confronted with it on a daily basis.

Is there any way we could get this chapter read out on Dave?

12

EYEBROW ASH SPECIAL

Like we all do, I often imagine how my life would have been if I had followed an alternative path. Some of you might wonder where you would be if you had worked harder at school, followed the love of your life to Mauritius or started keeping a pet rat. For me, these flights of fancy are often career-based. Don't get it twisted, I love being a comedian. I'm one of the fortunate few who has managed to follow a hobby and a passion all the way until it has become my job. But a job it is, so it does have its occasional moments of drudgery, when I allow myself the odd thought exercise on what could've been.

As I hope I've established by now, my other true love is food. So, I often think about what would've happened if I'd pursued that passion instead. What if I had become a chef? These fantasies are always short-lived. Being a chef in a professional kitchen is totally unlike being one in your own: it's high-pressured, competitive, and requires years of exacting and hard work to get to any sort of level. Even a cursory examination of my attempts at cooking at home will demonstrate why I should never be allowed to cook for actual customers. I am stroppy and petulant and will throw my toys out of the pram at the slightest hint of a mistake. You could call me a perfectionist, but this seems far too complimentary a term. A perfectionist suggests someone who has mastered their craft through failure and now holds themselves to a high standard. I expect to be perfect at things when I am trying them for the first time, and if I'm not I throw a wobbly. I'm not a perfectionist. I am at best deluded, and at worst a big baby.

Cooking at home is when I most often act out these ugly character traits. What's worse is, I never learn. Every time I go in all guns blazing expecting to produce Michelin-star-level cuisine, inevitably fail, and spend the next few days miserable. This is a depressingly regular event. I set out with the best intentions. 'This time,' I tell myself, 'I am going to be an oasis of calm in the kitchen. Something will probably go wrong, and you know what? That's fine. I'm not on *MasterChef*. I can just roll with it.' It's a promise I have yet to keep.

I sometimes wish that recipe books would be more honest about the real home cook's experience. They present everything as if it's super simple and only an idiot could screw it up. Ergo, I screw it up and feel like an idiot. What we need is a little bit of realism from the food publishing world. With that in mind, here is a groundbreaking presentation of what I like to call 'Ed's Special Lasagne'.

ED'S SPECIAL LASAGNE

Ingredients

Olive oil, onion, garlic, beef mince, pork mince, red wine, chopped tomatoes, tomato purée, low self-esteem, flour, butter, milk, a short temper, lasagne sheets, mozzarella, Cheddar, Parmesan, a terrible oven, a blunt knife, deep-rooted anger about father.

Method

First, dice the onion. 'Dice' is a cooking word that means 'chop', and despite it being called 'dice', you need to make the bits smaller than actual dice. There are many ways of successfully dicing an onion, but for this recipe you need to ignore all of them and wildly hack at the onion until it is in a range of different-sized pieces. This ensures uneven cooking and an unpleasant eating experience.

Finely grate the garlic into a paste. You know you've finished when you feel the unimaginable pain of grating your finger. The skin and blood adds depth of flavour. Once you realize all the garlic is stuck on the back of the grater, smack it on to the side of a ceramic bowl to release it, shattering the bowl and somehow leaving the garlic where it was. Use your bloody finger and flick it directly on to the floor.

Gently brown the beef and pork mince in olive oil. If you can't achieve an all-over brown colour, burn some and leave some raw - that still means they are all brown on average. The mince will be producing a lot of liquid. Momentarily consider taking a shot of it just to see what would happen.

Add the onions and garlic, making sure to get at least half of the onions on to the hob's flame. The acrid smell will keep any nosey people out of the kitchen! Add a splash of red wine, then drink the rest of the red wine. Add the tomatoes and the purée, then wash the can ready for recycling. Forget about that and put it in the normal bin. Let the sauce simmer until it looks like food.

Now prepare the béchamel. Throughout this process, continue to swear and scream about why you didn't just buy a jar. Combine the flour and butter to make a roux, then slowly whisk in the milk over a gentle heat until you have a silky-smooth sauce that coats the back of the spoon. Once you have hit this point, add some more flour to thicken it, and create huge lumps. Then leave on the heat while you go for an emergency shit, and return to the pan to find a brown mess. Better than two brown messes, am I right?! Ha ha, you're quite drunk now! Throw out the béchamel and just use mayonnaise or yoghurt.

Now it's time to build the lasagne. Garfield likes lasagne, doesn't he? Take a few minutes to be reminded of your cat that died, and cry. At this point, realize that you don't have a proper dish for the lasagne, and instead decide to bake it in a muffin tin. Layer up meat sauce, pasta sheets, béchamel and mountains of cheese until you have run out.

Make sure you have not preheated your oven, and pop your meaty muffins in. To make up for lack of preheating, whack oven up to full, then realize you've actually put the grill on. You've scorched the tops of your pasta until what you have made is closer to a crème brûlée than a lasagne. Turn off the oven, fall asleep in front of it, and *voilà*! A very special lasagne.

During the first Covid lockdown, my obsession with barbecues (see Chapter 2) hit a new high and I decided it was a wonderful time to become a master of Texas-style slow-smoked brisket. Well, as per, I decided that I would be a master immediately. I spent far too much on a huge piece of meat and set up the barbecue to smoke it over a long period of time. And I mean a *long* period of time. In typical fashion, I bought a Bluetooth-enabled meat thermometer, so I could keep an eye on how the meat was doing during the entire process. I quickly realized, though, that as it was Bluetooth, I couldn't actually leave the immediate perimeter of the meat. So, there I sat. For twelve hours.

When I opened the lid of the barbecue, I was greeted by what I can only describe as a smoker's lung. My panic tantrum started to set in. I managed to calm myself down somehow. 'It's all about the taste,' I thought. 'As long as it's juicy, all will be well.'

Let me tell you, you have never seen anything as dry as that meat. As I cut into it, the famously dry raconteur and author Will Self walked by and commented, 'That looks a bit dry.' At one point, I thought I saw a bit of liquid, but that turned out to be a mirage. It ended as many of my cooking attempts do. A lot of shouting, food in the bin.

Last Christmas, we were at my mum's house. I used to be happy with letting her get on with the cooking. She's a great cook, particularly of roast potatoes. Like most pathetic British mummy's boys, I truly believe that my mum's roast potatoes are the best. It's not something I say just because she is my mum. I truly, deep down in my heart, believe that hers would stand up against any professional chef's. Despite all this, of late I cannot help but be an annoying presence in the kitchen on Christmas Day, picking over what she is doing and making 'helpful' suggestions. For decades my mother has made delicious Christmas dinners, but now I have decided that they can be improved by me gently nudging her to follow tips I saw on a YouTube video three days earlier. She rightly doesn't budge.

As a concession last year, she allowed me one job. All I had to do was light the brandy on the Christmas pudding. A simple job, you would've thought, for someone so versed in flaming cocktails. It should have been a fairly easy process – you warm some brandy, tip it on the pudding and light it. What I chose to do was warm the brandy and light it in the pan, while staring intently at it with my face wedged over the top of the liquid. The whoosh of flames engulfed my face, removing every single last hair of my eyebrows. I don't know if you've ever tried to have a tantrum with no eyebrows, but it's very difficult for people to take you seriously. Next time someone is angry, I urge you to imagine them with no eyebrows. It really takes the tension out of the situation. The upshot was I had a nightmare and everyone else had a lovely Christmas laugh. They soon stopped laughing when they started eating the pudding, which was covered in eyebrow ash.

Despite my constant reminders to myself that I should be more realistic about my abilities in the kitchen, during the first Covid lockdown I decided that I would make potato dauphinoise for the first time, and that it would be the perfect potato dauphinoise. It was also to be the day that I used a mandolin for the first time. That's a piece of kitchen equipment, by the way, and nothing to do with Captain Corelli. It's not beyond the realms of possibility that I would try to master a potato dish and a musical instrument simultaneously, but on this day I was focusing solely on the potatoes.

A mandolin is a notoriously dangerous kitchen tool. You may have seen one. It looks innocuous enough, like a plastic plank with a blade in the middle. The aim is to stroke whatever you are cutting downwards over the blade, producing uniform and thin slices. Perfect for today, I thought. It's also essential you use the provided guard, which sits on top of your chosen ingredient and protects your fingers from the impossibly sharp blade. I popped the guard to one side and got on with slicing. Within seconds, the potato had slipped out of my hand and I had hacked off half of my thumb knuckle. My wife correctly pointed out that it was bleeding so profusely that we should go to A&E. I pointed out that I couldn't feel any pain, because I was too devastated that I had got it wrong. I proceeded to elevate the wound and tried to finish the dish one-handed.

After an hour of this, she dragged me to Casualty. Of course, given when this occurred, the NHS was hugely overstretched. It was embarrassing enough that I was going to hospital with such a middle-class injury, but to do so during a national health crisis? I was ready to die on the spot. Which would've, ironically, made their job even harder. I do think there should be a separate department for preventable middle-class accidents. If you've injured yourself while making potato dauphinoise or got some Farrow & Ball paint in your eye, you do not deserve to be seen alongside people who have genuine medical concerns. You should be made to wait for eight hours, be given a prescription for some perspective and then bundled out the door. As it was, I needed eight stitches and now have a permanent scar. This was nothing compared to the potato dauphinoise. It ended up having so much blood in it that only a vampire would have been interested. The tragedy is, the dish had been spiked with such a large amount of garlic that my only customer would have also run for the hills.

I think it's clear why my temperament means that I am not cut out to work in a kitchen. I am stroppy, quick to anger and childish. The only option I can see for myself is to become a head chef.

SPICE

No, this is not a section about the illegal drug Spice. Illegal drugs have no place in a book about food. I am not, nor have I ever been, a drughead. Why would I be? I have cheese, remember? Good food brings me all the highs I need on a daily basis, thank you very much. I simply do not have time in my life to be focusing on chasing the dragon; I'm far too busy thinking about what I'm going to prepare for lunch. Most of the drug people I know don't seem to care about what they eat. They are, in the main, skinny minnies who seem only to obsess about where their next sweet fix is coming from.

Marijuana is different, of course. The weed-men get something called 'the munchies', which seems to increase their appetite. It does not, however, increase the discernment of their palates. They will shove anything in their jazzed-up gobs, desperate to fill the hole the potent Mary Jane has left in their souls. They seem to favour low-grade snack foods, often crisps made of potato substitute, the kind of thing that if I had my way would be banned from production. Wotsits, Monster Munch, Space Raiders. Those are the chosen nibbles for your average stoner. Frankly, if a crisp is not made of potato, you will not find it in my house unless it is being used as a no-doubt-effective cat litter. Even then it would not be safe from the smokers. They would eat from the bottom of a cat's toilet quicker than you can say 'Cut your hair and wash your clothes, you big hippy.'

No, I am of course talking about the real meaning of spice, before it was co-opted by criminals. I love spicy food. In many ways, it does provide me with the sort of high that one might get from something more nefarious. A perfectly pitched hot and spicy dish can be transportive, making my face flush and my head tingle, and making me feel like I'm being gently warmed by an open fire. I've only lately discovered Szechuan cuisine, which can have the incredible effect of numbing the mouth, like you're at the dentist, but a delicious Chinese one. The first time I tried it, I thought I was having an allergic reaction, or that a wasp had flown on to my plate and I had swallowed it. I'm not doing a great job of selling it. Very rarely when someone is recommending you food will they include the words 'dentist' and 'wasp'. But take my word for it. Get yourself down to a wasp dentist restaurant at the first available opportunity.

Yes, I love spicy food, but it has taken me a while to know my limits. In much the same way as alcohol, for a long time the notion of spice and chilli was tied up with some form of twisted masculinity, as it is for many men. I thought that the hotter the food I could handle, the harder I was. Forgetting, as with beer, that I should perhaps be prioritizing having a pleasant experience rather than impressing someone who doesn't care or doesn't exist. This attitude has got me into trouble multiple times in the past.

When I was sixteen, I was in Brazil on holiday with my dad, stepmother, brother and sister. We were eating in a remote restaurant that was essentially a lady's house. She had prepared us a fantastic home-cooked meal, and being me, I wolfed down the first portion and went for seconds. That's where I was as a person at the time. The first portion was merely something to get out of the way, something to line my stomach for the more important helpings to come. Available as a condiment was a bottle of vinegar that was filled to the brim with small, brutal-looking chillies. I had tried it with the first helping, but by the time it came to the second I was ready to go all in. I upended the bottle above the plate, not realizing that someone had loosened the lid. The entirety of the bottle, chillies and all, gushed all over my Brazilian stew.

A sensible man might have just left the food. However, as we were basically in a woman's home, my dad implored me to eat it so as not to be wasteful or rude. I was simultaneously powered by a belief that I was some sort of chilli-based Danny Dyer hard nut, so I did. Every bite was agony. I ended up eating the whole plate squatting on the floor screaming and red-faced, downing lager as if I were at a stag do in Ibiza. My family, of course, did their bit to help with screaming laughter. Not just for the duration of the meal, but to the present day. It still gets brought up at every family event.

I'm not one to learn from such an experience. Years later, in LA, I went into a taco restaurant that had been recommended to me and ordered a taco that came with not only a warning but also a sliding scale of chilli heat that went from one to five. I ordered a number two, and the man refused to serve me. That is how white I am. I walked in, he clocked me, and he immediately decided that he would rather refuse me service than endanger me. Me being me, I insisted. We compromised on a level one taco. I took one bite, immediately felt like I was going to pass out, faked getting a phone call and left to heave over a bin in full view of the restaurant. I can only speculate on what number five would've done, but I'd imagine it would've been like my first run all over again. Not only will I never go back to that place, I doubt I will ever gather the bravery to go back to the state of California.

At the Mach Comedy Festival in Wales, there is a curry van that I frequent every year. On one occasion, I saw Nish

Kumar eating a type of curry that I never saw them serve to anyone else. When I enquired what it was, he told me it was a special extra-spicy curry that they had prepared just for him because they knew he could handle it. Now, I'm not one to stand for this kind of racial-based injustice, so I immediately demanded he let me try some. Instant mistake. I felt like someone had put a cactus in my throat and then a slightly bigger cactus up my anus. Unbelievably, despite seeing me in the worst state of my life, my wife also decided to lick the spoon. Charlie is worse with spice than I am, and it sent her running to the bar for water, where the staff assumed she was having a panic attack. I'll say it, guys: sometimes, white people shouldn't be allowed things.

Nowadays, I value flavour over power. It took me a while, but I got there. I no longer order based purely on the number of cartoon chillies next to a dish name, and when I home-cook I'm always careful to use spice to enhance rather than destroy the flavour of the main ingredients. Ultra-spicy things tend to give me insanely squeaky hiccups anyway. There is no greater fall from grace to witness than watching a puffed-up and proud man embark on eating something spicy with the arrogant air of a superhero, only to be reduced to making the sound of a cat trapped in a door.

There is some latent part of me, though, that is still tempted by those challenges that some restaurants have. You know the ones. 'Hottest wings in the world! If you finish them, you get them free!' This is a false economy. You can inflict great pain on yourself, and what do you gain? At best, nothing more than a T-shirt proclaiming what a tit you are. At worst, a hole in your oesophagus. Yet still I am tempted. It might kill me, but it would be quite the way to go! Maybe I'll try it. I'm sure it would help push this book.

You'll know by now if I went ahead with another challenge. You're either reading a book written by a comedian with a podcast, or the final words of the man from the news who died hiccuping in a roadside diner. Both options are equally undignified, if you ask me.

13

THE BIG D

If you have listened to the *Off Menu* podcast, you'll know that I am not the resident dessert obsessive. James Acaster loves desserts to the extent that it is a diagnosable illness. Because of this, I think my enjoyment of all things sweet is slightly overshadowed. I love desserts too, guys! I just don't think about them every waking moment. They are not a one hundred per cent necessity to me.

The way I see it, if I get to the end of a meal and I feel like having a dessert, I have not done a good enough job on the savoury courses. The dream home-cooked or restaurant meal for me is when I have eaten so much by way of starters and mains that I absolutely cannot stomach the idea of any more food. Why would I limit myself at the start of the meal in order to leave room for something at the end? I live in the moment. *Carpe diem!* I do not procrastinate my carnal desires. Making yourself wait until the end of the meal to truly indulge is a tantric form of eating that is complete anathema to someone like me. The starters and mains should not be foreplay, they are the main event. Desserts are like cuddling afterwards (sometimes I want to, but sometimes I am too ashamed and have to leave).

This is not to say that I don't enjoy them, or that they can't be a wonderfully complementary end to a particular meal. I've just always been more savoury-focused, even as a child. We think of kids as being sugar and pudding obsessed, but this was never me. I was always happier gnawing on a bit of cheese or meat, like a dog at a medieval banquet. While all my friends went gaga for sweeties, I was the one much more into exploring the glorious world of the savoury. Pick 'n' mix to most children is a dream come true, while I would stand there imagining a better world where the sections were filled to the brim with charcuterie from around the world. Even the desserts I do enjoy tend to have some sort of savoury element.

I was once at my dad's house and found him in the kitchen spitting something into the bin. He'd been making a meringue, and in a move very unlike him had used salt instead of sugar. Of course, I found this hilarious. It's the sort of thing that would happen in a bad family sitcom, and I challenge you to imagine anything funnier than your own dad spitting into a bin. It's probably the most undignified thing anyone can do. He was so disgusted by what he had cooked because of a silly mistake that he had to put his face right next to the bin where rubbish lives. Brilliant.

I say that that is the most undignified thing anyone could do, but I immediately topped it. He had left the meringue on the side in the kitchen. Of course, I tried it. I didn't get where I am today without putting everything in my mouth regardless of warning signs. How else do you learn? Well, on this occasion I learnt nothing other than that I like salty meringue. Yes, it was overpowering and yes, it made my face pucker like a dying slug, but I loved it. This is how I've always been. What I crave on an hourly basis is salt and fat.

Salted caramel, in my opinion, is the greatest invention since the internet. Finally, it seems, even the dessert guys are coming round to my kind of thinking. It must've been invented by accident. In fact, my dad was on the right track. If he had not shamefully started bin-gobbing, he could've worked on what he created and eventually become the next Willy Wonka. As it is, it was left to someone else to discover the joy of salted caramel. I'd imagine that person is absolutely loaded now, laughing to themselves all day about the fact that a domestic kitchen disaster has led to their sticky empire. Hopefully one day I will be able to follow in their footsteps – but I'm sad to report that thus far my experiments with chilli trifle, mutton cupcakes and garlic tiramisu have been a complete and utter failure. It's actually quite hard to find normal caramel now. I remember a time when salted caramel was a rare novelty, but now? You'll be lucky to find the OG caramel. Soon, normal caramel will be a distant memory, only to be resurrected in twenty years by a new generation of food hipsters who claim it's better. It will follow the same trajectory as vinyl records, and you know what? I will fall for it, despite knowing deep down that it is bullshit.

Even dripping with salted caramel, broadly I'd say that any dessert that doesn't feature chocolate and/or peanut butter is pointless. It's no coincidence that these two things are probably the two most calorie-dense substances on the planet. This is what my body is always desperate for. I want as much fat and calories as I can pack in as quickly and as deliciously as possible. I don't know why this is. It just feels deep within me, a primal urge. Perhaps it is some historical caveman impulse. I am so desperate to survive cold winters that all I want to eat are things that give me a thick fatty coat.

It's certainly not the case for everyone. I've even met people who don't like chocolate. These people are out there, and they should be avoided at all costs, as they are quite frankly Patrick Bateman-level psychopaths. They are not *trying* to avoid chocolate, they actively *want* to avoid chocolate. They're normally the sort of people who get up early and do sit-ups. If someone doesn't like chocolate, I assume they have something very dark going on in their private lives. They must be getting their buzz from somewhere. If I was brave enough, as soon as I discovered somebody who doesn't like chocolate I would call in an anonymous tip to the police to search their basement. Nine out of ten times, there would be bodies.

Chocolate has been one of the biggest loves of my life for as long as I can remember. This stands to reason. As you know, cheese is my favourite thing, and chocolate is basically pudding cheese. I don't remember the first time I had it, but it must've been one of my first solid foods. I was hooked. So much so, I'm annoyed I didn't get to eat it earlier in my

life. If I was given my time as a baby again, I would abandon my mother and latch on to the Nesquik bunny for
sustenance. (I've just looked it up, and it appears that the
Nesquik bunny is male, so this wouldn't have been possible.
Even if the bunny was female, I'm presuming that she would
produce chocolate breast milk, which feels inaccurate. I
think the bunny just likes Nesquik, rather than actually
having Nesquik as part of their reproductive physiology.
Glad we straightened that out.) Even now, in my calmer
eating days, I cannot eat chocolate at home without going
through the whole bar. I'm talking the big bars, by the way.
The individual-sized bars would never make it to my house.
They are devoured before I've even set foot outside the
newsagent's, or on rare occasions before I've made it to the
till. You've never seen anyone more baffled than a shopkeeper scanning an empty KitKat Chunky wrapper while
you profusely apologize with your mouth full.

As far as I can see it, this is one of the only reasons to
have a child. I'm always so jealous in a supermarket when I
see a little kid sitting in a trolley, munching on a sweet treat
that has not been paid for yet. There's a certain amount of
trust given to parents in this situation. The store turns a
blind eye to the consumption of goods before they reach
the till, as they are keeping the child quiet. It's then assumed
that the responsible adult will have the empty packet
scanned through later and will pay for it as normal. There's
an understanding that the parents themselves will not
join in with this behaviour. Not if I had a child. I'd be tucking straight into a big cookie to power me through the

shopping. Then, when it came to paying, I would gesture to my child and say something like 'Sorry, he's a greedy little bastard' before wiping crumbs away from my mouth.

Until that day, I'm sticking to my big bars of Dairy Milk, or more recently Tony's Chocolonely, which they optimistically divide into squares. These squares, as far as I can work out, are there as guides to portion size. These manufacturers are either very dumb or very stupid. I'm not using those tiny squares. How many squares do they imagine I will have? One? A line? It's unclear, but what I do know is that to prove a point, I will just bite into the bar across all the squares. Portioning large chocolate bars is a complete waste of money and no doubt an unnecessary blight on the environment. If the chocolate companies stuck to making these bars in the most efficient way (as one smooth slab designed for one person) then we could put off global warming by at least fifty years.

The existence of squares, unfortunately, suggests the existence of people who eat just one square. These are probably the same buzz-killing puritans who only have one drink. They are potentially worse than people who don't eat chocolate at all. They clearly like the stuff, but they seem perfectly satisfied with one tiny stamp-sized morsel before they put the packet away and probably exclaim something like 'Oh, I'm such a naughty chocoholic!' No, you are not. You are not a chocoholic if you eat an amount that wouldn't even kill a dog. You are not a chocoholic if you make a bar last two weeks. You are not a chocoholic if you say things like 'I just let a square melt in my mouth and really experience the flavour.' You are an imposter. If you were a character in *Willy Wonka and the Chocolate Factory*, by the time you found the golden ticket the tour would've already happened.

You might think I'm on the path to launching a diatribe against people who like dark chocolate. The 'healthy' chocolate. This would be the populist thing to do. Well, sorry, I love dark chocolate. I love all chocolate, and I mean *all* chocolate. No level of dark will put me off, as long as I'm getting that cocoa hit. I've been known, now and again, to eat 100 per cent dark. I see it as a nod towards my former teen goth identity. It's the most heavy metal of all the chocolates. It's incredibly bitter and has so little sugar that it could probably be considered to be beef jerky. The myth about dark chocolate is that you can be satisfied with less. That you can have one square, enjoy the experience, and then not want any more. Well, call me a myth-buster. Because I will hammer down a dark bar at the same rate as a regular person would drink a glass of water.

Dark chocolate poses no threat to me. Nothing can stop the relentless march of my chocoholism. Some people claim to be 'chocoholics' in a light-hearted way. But they do not know the meaning of addiction. I have chocoholism. I'll eat the coating from a chocolate raisin and throw the raisin away. I'll lick the foil of a bar, so as not to waste those final few specks of choc dust. I'll eat chocolate when it gets that weird white stuff on it. I'll order a cappuccino simply to suck the dust off the top. I'll eat dog chocolate. This is the true face of chocoholism, and if you can't cope with the reality of this, then you are not a chocoholic. You are a fraud.

With all this chocolate chat, many of you will be thinking that I am continuing to fail to cover something about myself that is quite important. That I'm putting off the inevitable discussion. Well, here goes.

THE INEVITABLE DISCUSSION

We've left it long enough. All this talk of sugar, and I have barely even mentioned it. I am type 1 diabetic. I'm assuming that a lot of you knew this, given how often I am accused of bringing it up. I actually think in this book so far I have been quite restrained with references to my condition. Gold star, please! This is a food book and type 1 affects my eating at every juncture, so to leave it until now is admirable, to say the least. The fact is, I have been holding back so I could write a whole chapter about it. You thought you got away with it, didn't you? Well, bad luck, suckers! You're too deep in now! I even lulled you into a false sense of security by talking about chocolate for a few pages! 'Oh, he's on desserts and chocolate and he hasn't banged on about his diabetes yet . . . that's a relief.' Well, we're here now, and you have to look interested, otherwise you are committing a hate crime.

Quite why you might have thought I wouldn't bring it up is a mystery. It is one of my only defining characteristics as a comedian. I am a white, straight, privileged cis man who has had very little hardship in his life. Audiences have heard from people like me for years. Diabetes is one of my only fresh angles and I intend to exploit it until I die. I'm going to wring that pancreas dry.

DIAB-ORIGINS

I was first diagnosed in 1999, when I was thirteen. My diabetes origin story is not an exciting one. I didn't end up in hospital and I wasn't bitten by a radioactive Mars bar. In many ways, I was very lucky. My mum used to be a nurse, and as such she spotted symptoms early enough to take me to the GP before everything deteriorated to a dangerous level. Many people aren't so lucky to have a qualified medical professional in the house, so end up not seeing the signs and have to be admitted. This must be hugely scary, and I am forever grateful that my mum was so across it. It would be remiss of me at this stage not to at least mention the symptoms. Even if this book does nothing else, if it helps diagnose one person with type 1, it will have been worth it. Plus, that would do wonders for the publicity campaign. Just imagine the headlines!

'New book saves a life!'

'Ed Gamble's book had me dying of laughter, but then stopped me literally dying!'

'Curtis from Love Island *reveals he is diabetic!'*

So, here are the main symptoms of type 1 diabetes to keep an eye out for and get my book on the bestsellers list.

- *Feeling very thirsty* – my mum noticed I was drinking huge amounts of water. I was guzzling the stuff day and night. This is perhaps the only time of my life when she has ever suggested drinking one alcoholic beverage for every two waters. We should all healthily hydrate, of course, but what I was doing was outrageous. If you notice someone close to you glugging at an insane rate, urge them to go to a GP. They either have diabetes, rabies, or are turning into a mermaid. In all instances, they need to speak to a professional.

- *Urinating more often* – this is as a result partly of the increased thirst, but also the body desperately trying to rid itself of all the sugar that your muscles can't use thanks to your inability to produce insulin. Yet again, my mum noticed. I was up all hours of the night to use the toilet. Not that my mum was counting my wees. It just got to the point that it became obvious. I'm not suggesting you keep a spreadsheet of your family's pisses. If you did, though, it might be helpful. Even if you didn't find out anything medical, you could turn it into a fun game on Christmas Day and have a sweepstake on who went for a pee the most that year.

- *Weight loss* – before my diagnosis is actually the first time I lost weight without trying. I have to say, I couldn't help but feel slightly insulted that my mum immediately called this as being the result of a medical emergency rather than me finally blossoming into my skinny adult life. She was right to though. I was a traditionally fat child who ate a lot, so the fact that I hadn't changed my lifestyle at all but was still losing weight rang some alarm bells.

- *Being so sexy and a funny comedian* – if you are a very sexy and funny comedian, you are almost certainly type 1 diabetic. I can't think of any who aren't. Go to your GP immediately. Once they have stopped laughing and trying to have a kiss with you, they will diagnose you without even needing to do a blood test.

I was duly whisked off to my GP, who sent me for blood tests. A few days later, I was officially declared a type 1 diabetic. 'Declared' is possibly too grand a word for how it went down. I wasn't knighted with a big KitKat. I was sat down in his office and he patronizingly explained that I had 'this thing called diabetes'. The way he did this still rattles around my brain now and again. It was as if he was explaining it to a toddler.

This is one of the reasons why being diagnosed as a teenager is rough. In my mind, aged thirteen, I was an adult. To be spoken to like a child was quite disconcerting at what was already a stressful time. I wasn't a child, I thought. I could get a bus on my own and I'd snuck into *Cruel Intentions* at the cinema; surely I could be respected when it came to medical matters?

This extended to how I was initially treated within the NHS. As a thirteen-year-old, I fell into the bracket of a child. As such, I was the responsibility of the paediatrics department. My first hospital diabetic appointment felt humiliating. I was sat in a waiting room among eight- and nine-year-olds, on a blue plastic chair much too small for my ample teenage frame. It must've looked hilarious, but at the time it was very difficult to see the innate slapstick in something so life-changing. The walls were covered in colourful cartoon characters designed to soothe the children and make it less of a jarring experience. But I was a teenager and I found it patronizing. Why not put some stuff on the wall that would make me feel comfortable? A Slipknot poster, or some light pornography? Nothing too graphic, but at the very least a Rachel Stevens *FHM* shoot.

Even the equipment they used was tooled towards children, sometimes in quite a sinister way. The first time I had a blood test at the hospital, it was a fairly harrowing experience. They took a while to find a vein, which was bad enough. It took so long, the nurse looked like she was starting to doubt I had any. This would've been a real revelation in the medical field. I had gone in there as a new diabetic, and I would've come out as a case study. A lifelong, lifestyle-altering condition was bad enough, but to find out that I had no vascular system? No, thanks. Eventually, they had to use a tourniquet-style elasticated strap. That sounds fine, but in an effort to make it more child-friendly, the strap was decorated . . . with cartoon vampires. Quite how this is supposed to relax children, I have no idea. Vampires are famously monstrous and evil creatures, obsessed with drinking blood. For a child seeing this, their minds would've gone wild. Not only are they in the scary situation of having blood taken, but now there is also a suggestion that the blood is being taken for a demonic entity to drink. Why else would there be vampires on the tourniquet? Clearly they ran the hospital as a sort of buffet and couldn't help but add their image to the paraphernalia, as one final satanic cackle at their victims. Maybe some of the other patients had less of an active imagination than I did, but I do think they would've been better off with images of Rachel Stevens here as well.

As much as I found being in the children's ward uncomfortable, I do think decorating hospitals should carry on into adult treatment. When I aged out of the paediatrics department, I was thrown headlong into the world of the adult wards. I had never spent much time in hospital up until this point, so finding out how miserable it really is in these places was a shock. There was no effort to make the surroundings relaxing or comforting, as there had been for the younger patients. My only real understanding of hospital life back then had been watching *Carry On* films on Saturday afternoons. The reality, you'll be shocked to hear, was far from this. There were no saucy innuendos, cheeky flings or filthy old men becoming involved with unfeasibly attractive younger women. The overwhelming feeling in most of the rooms was 'beige', apart from the occasional room which bucked the trend and went with 'grey'. At an already dark time of my life, this made everything seem a little bit bleaker.

I'm not suggesting a complete redesign, don't get me wrong. As I write this, the NHS is under extreme pressure and it shouldn't be using its scant budget on installing fountains or Japanese Zen gardens (however nice this would be). Let's get some stuff on the walls though, shall we? Yes, I know there are often posters up, but these tend to be about illnesses you don't even have. There is nothing more disconcerting than sitting in a hospital waiting room for one problem while reading symptoms for another. Twenty minutes in, I normally convince myself that not only am I type 1 diabetic, but I also have pneumonia and endometriosis. The children get cartoons on the wall, or drawings that they themselves have done. So let's get some pictures up that middle-aged people enjoy. Catalogue shots of ovens, or a photo of Sir David Attenborough? Or better yet, cover up some of the damp patches with estate agent listings for houses that are far outside everyone's price range so we can simultaneously tut at the price of property while also secretly fantasizing about living there. That would certainly have helped to allay some of my nervousness as I prepared to be poked and prodded in a grim white shell of a room by a tired-looking doctor.

It occurs to me as I write this that it's all very well explaining my journey in diabetes, but there will be plenty of you who don't actually know what it is. In order to talk about how it affects my relationship with food (which is of course why I'm bringing it up), let's get this bit out of the way.

THE SCIENCE BIT

There may, of course, be people reading this who know the basics of what type 1 diabetes actually is, but given encounters I have had in the past, there are also a lot of people out there who have no idea. These people tend to think it is something to do with too much sugar or not enough sugar. I have no hard feelings towards these people, by the way – I don't expect everyone to know the intricate details of what is a very difficult condition to get to grips with. Before I was diagnosed, my only encounter with diabetes had been Danni from *Neighbours*. She kept some chocolate bars in a pencil case, which some bullies stole and wouldn't give her back. So, in my mind, type 1 diabetics were Australians who loved chocolate and didn't have many pens. I've since been forced to learn about the condition, of course, by virtue of having it.

We should get the factual stuff done before this turns into a TED talk. In type 1 diabetics, the beta cells in the pancreas that produce insulin have been destroyed by our own immune systems. Insulin is the hormone that helps regulate blood glucose level. When normies eat something, their pancreas releases insulin, which helps the body use that sugar as energy for the muscles. If you are a type 1 diabetic chosen by God, you no longer produce insulin, meaning that you have to inject your own. Essentially, you have to manually take over one of your body's processes in order to stay alive. Untreated, it means all that glucose stays swimming around in your blood which can cause comas, even death. At the very worst, you can turn into Bertie Bassett.

In my capacity as a judge on the *Great British Menu*, this is of course a line I have to walk regularly. The savoury courses are normally a fairly sedate affair, medically speaking, but the desserts are a different beast altogether. The real challenge comes in finals week, when the best chefs of the series come together and battle it out to see who will reach the banquet – the reason why they are all competing. In that week, we as judges eat eight meals a day, divided by course. This means that for one Friday a year, I have to eat eight desserts in a six-hour period. This, for a diabetic, is completely unhinged. I want to use my platform to prove that type 1 diabetics can eat what everyone eats, that our condition does not limit us in any way. The catch here being that, frankly, absolutely nobody would ever sit down and eat that amount of sugar in such a short period of time. I am proving that a type 1 diabetic can handle a situation that absolutely no non-diabetic would ever attempt. It doesn't always pay off. As you eat more sugar, you have to inject more and more insulin, and that can stack its effect and you can actually end up with a low blood glucose level. Yes, on more than one occasion while filming I have come to the end of an eight-dessert day and had to eat some sugar. The camera crew must think I am insane.

The Types

I'm always very specific when I talk about the type of diabetes that I have. I am a type 1 diabetic. We are in the minority when it comes to diabetes, and I can't say that I'm not oddly proud that we still get the number 1. There's fewer of us and we are still ranked on the top of the podium. It's very much the hipster diabetes. It means, as I said, that my pancreas no longer produces insulin, because the beta cells have been destroyed by my immune system. That's right, my immune system is a hard nut. Not only did it endeavour to fight off colds and illnesses, it also went one step further and started attacking my own body. If you see the immune system as a bouncer, mine worked on the door keeping out troublesome patrons before going into the nightclub and killing all the staff.

Type 2 is distinctly different, which is why it annoys all of us when the media simply refers to 'diabetes'. I can't speak to the intricacies of the condition in the same way as I can about type 1. As far as I'm aware, there weren't any characters in *Neighbours* with type 2 diabetes – certainly none who featured in a central plotline. I guess it's just less glamorous. Sorry, type 2s – no soap operas for your gang. In type 2, the body largely still produces some insulin, if less. There also may be an increase in insulin resistance, meaning that blood sugar levels will be higher. It can often be controlled with diet or tablets and can even be reversed in some cases. It's no fun and games, of course, but I hope we can agree that us type 1s are way more hardcore. We are the Bear Grylls of pancreatic issues. We are lifers, sticking ourselves with needles on a daily basis. Type 1 4 Life.

The thing I do not envy about type 2, however, is the way that it is portrayed in the media. In some instances, type 2 can be caused by an unhealthy lifestyle or obesity, but this is not always the case. Age and genetics are also big factors, but this doesn't grab the headlines. As such, type 2 sufferers are often painted as being lazy and overweight – meaning that they are seen as being at fault for their own condition and costing the NHS money. This is very unfair. For a start, lifestyle and weight are not always in people's control economically or genetically. Secondly, there are many other things that can cause type 2. Sadly, painting with broad brushstrokes is the way the media likes to work, and this is the easiest route for them. Shamefully, I have been guilty of doing that myself in the past.

I had a big stand-up routine about being type 1, which was inspired by a trip I took to New York with friends for New Year's Eve 2017/18. The day before we were due to come home, there was a blizzard the likes of which I had never seen before. The city was completely whited out with swirling tornados of snow, which was exciting at the time. It didn't stop us walking miles to go to restaurants, of course. We just had to do our best impression of Ernest

Shackleton and wrap up warm and hike from block to block to make it to a diner we had found on Google, only to find out it was shut because none of the staff were as stupid as us to be out in the storm.

It became less exciting when our flight home was cancelled, and we found out we would have to stay an extra week. I loved it in New York, but I had definitely allotted a certain amount of brain time for the trip which was due to run out on that planned flight home. There's only so much nightly drinking and eating as if you are on Death Row the body can cope with. Being comedians, we all tweeted about our situation, desperate for attention, validation and sympathy. What we hadn't considered was the media actually picking up on it. A combination of January being a slow news month and the fact that we were in entertainment meant that our predicament actually made the news cycle. It was on the BBC website, and Lloyd Langford and John Robins were interviewed on Sky News (Lloyd choosing to remain slack-jawed and silent throughout, while wearing a necklace that said 'USA' which he had found in a drawer in our Airbnb).

The BBC news article was the one that sparked the routine. While introducing the rest of the comics to their readers via their professional credits, the journalist chose to describe me as a 'diabetic comedian'. This was almost certainly done with a heavy dose of knowing humour. I've since met the journalist and he confirmed this. At the time, though, I had no idea if he meant it to be funny or not. It made me laugh, though, and I decided it would be a great jumping-off point for one of my famously loud routines. I expressed dissatisfaction with the label, and it allowed me to write about diabetes in a way I hadn't quite managed before.

Within this, though, I talked about the types of diabetes with a lot less accuracy and nuance than I have done in this book. I described type 2 diabetes as not counting because 'they did it to themselves'. A silly joke, I thought at the time. I still think there is something funny about me, a type 1 diabetic, starting beef with people with a different version of the same condition. But the way I did it, I now recognize, was not ideal. From an audience's perspective, I was amplifying a negative stereotype that people with the condition have to deal with every day. I did the joke on *Live at the Apollo*, spreading that stereotype even further. People lodged their complaints with me, explaining why it perhaps wasn't the best thing to say, regardless of my intent. I thought about it (ideally something I would've done before I wrote the joke) and removed it from my set.

That's the great thing about being a comedian. You can just stop doing a joke if you decide it is upsetting people and bringing no great good to the world. More people should do this. We live in a time when comedians seem to be worried that they are being censored and defensively double down on harmful jokes. This definitely crossed my mind, but after I broke through this instinct, I realized it was probably better for everyone to retire the line. It wasn't even that good a joke anyway.

MANAGEMENT

This may all sound fairly straightforward. It sounds like we just have to inject every day and everything is looked after, but this is far from the case. When your body does it naturally, it really is very good at it. It knows the exact amount of insulin it needs in collaboration with how much glucose it needs. When we have to take over, however, it's slightly more complicated. It's like being asked to take charge of the fuel injection system in your car while you are driving. Anything different you eat, environmental factors, your physical health, your mental health and even how much sleep you've had can affect how your body reacts to your treatment. It's a constant tightrope walk every day of checking your blood glucose levels, injecting insulin and correcting mistakes. I am fond of telling people it's like having an extra job twenty-four hours of the day, but I'm a comedian so, in reality, it's more like having one job.

Some days, my diabetes behaves itself. I need to do minimal testing and injections, and I can relegate it to the background of my thoughts, unencumbered as I go about my daily business. Often, though, it does not behave itself. My blood glucose levels will end up swooping. I'll eat something and inject insulin to control the spike that the food inevitably brings, but I won't give enough at the right time. This will send my blood sugar high. Then the insulin kicks in and it crashes low, meaning I have to take some sugar onboard. This might then send my levels high again, and the cycle resumes. This is tiring mentally as well as physically. A low blood glucose means I am shaky and weak, and a high blood sugar will make me sluggish and sad. It's a rollercoaster ride, but one where you feel terrible at all points, like most of the ones in Blackpool.

For a long time, I strived for perfection and associated my diabetic control with my own personality. If I had a bad day with it, I would blame myself and consider myself a failure. This is extremely unhelpful. While as diabetics we do need to be across the control and do our best, perfection is not possible. Certainly it does not mean that we have failed as people. I am not my diabetes; it is simply something I have to deal with. This is why I try to refer to it in the third person as much as possible. A while ago, however ridiculous this sounds, I started to think of it like a naughty puppy. It needs care and attention, but sometimes, no matter what you do, it will go mad and wee on the carpet. I can follow sensible courses of action and do all of the research, but my diabetes is a little terror and sometimes just has a mind of its own. All I need to do each time is learn something from the situation and try and employ it next time I find myself in the same circumstances.

Thinking of it as a puppy has certainly soothed some of my worries. I used to think of diabetes as something that was ravaging my body, that was controlling me. Now, I am the proud owner of a scruffy little Labrador, and to all intents and purposes I am in control. I may have taken this dog thought experiment too far – my wife regularly hears me exclaim things like 'Oh, you naughty little shit' or

'What are we going to do about you?' after I've seen that my blood glucose level isn't where I want it to be. Initially she thought I had lost my mind. Now she knows why I do it, she still thinks I have lost my mind. But it helps. Having a chronic condition can be daunting. There's no end in sight, and that can be an overwhelming feeling. We can all feel overwhelmed by things in life. I am no self-help guru, but at the very least I can recommend thinking of your problems as if they are a small dog.

When I was first diagnosed, I was told there would be a cure within ten years. I wish they hadn't said that. I was diagnosed in 1999. As you probably know, this cure is yet to emerge, and I'm not confident it will, certainly in my lifetime. What is more likely, I think, is the relentless march of medical technology getting us to the point where diabetics can live as close to a normal life as possible. Even in my time as a diabetic, things have come on leaps and bounds. Only a few years ago, if I wanted to test my blood glucose I would have had to prick my finger, extract blood and dab it on to a machine. Now there is technology available called a constant glucose monitor. This enables me literally to keep an eye on what my levels are on my phone at all times, see if they are dropping or escalating and do something about it before it becomes a problem. This seemed like a pipe dream when I was first diagnosed, but here we are, living in the future. There are multiple versions of this tech floating around, but it is an amazing thing. With a simple look at my screen, I can check where I'm at and whether I need to act on anything. In the main, though, it is a great excuse to be on my phone. If anyone accuses me of being rude, I can immediately throw egg on their faces by informing them that it is, in fact, a medical necessity. I live for the day when someone confronts me about it in the cinema. We all dream of being in arguments that we can definitely win, and this is mine.

FOOD AND DIABETES

I've spent a while talking about diabetes in general. 'This is a food book,' you might be thinking. 'Talk about pizza some more, you fraud!' Well, calm down. To me, diabetes is intrinsically linked with food, and I needed you to understand why. Everything I eat comes with extra decisions, much more so than when a normy eats. If you are reading this as a non-diabetic, first of all, congratulations. You have it so good. When you want to eat something, you decide what to eat and then you eat it. Then your body takes care of the rest. We're all very happy for you. When a type 1 diabetic eats, there are numerous factors to take into account, predictions to make and consequences to accept. It's a lot of work and brain power. How much insulin to inject, where our blood glucose level is sitting, what we are eating, whether we have exercised, and even the weather all play roles in this decision. And the twist? Even if we take all of these things on board, our decision may massively backfire and it could affect our energy levels and mood for the rest of the day, let alone our actual physical wellbeing short term or long term. For something that has had a lot of exact science invested into it over the years, being a diabetic is never an exact science.

Which makes my passion for food, if you think about it, even more admirable and heroic. Far be it from me to brand myself an inspiration and an icon, but I'm going to go ahead and do it anyway. It would probably be easier for me to eat the same thing every day. A certain level of predictability is good for diabetic control. Your body knows what to expect, and it reacts graciously. I could probably establish myself a diet that has minimal impact on my blood sugar levels, eat that repeatedly and maintain a very healthy lifestyle. But how boring does that sound? Food is my greatest joy. I love exploring food, trying new things and indulging. Diabetes, if you look at just the numbers, does not enjoy this. But I simply refuse to give in to the puppy. Relationships are about compromise, and I take the same attitude to my condition.

One of the prevailing myths about diabetes is that we cannot eat what we want. I've been at dinners with people when they suddenly panic when they offer me dessert. They retract the offer and say something like 'Oh God, I'm so sorry,' in a tone of voice usually reserved for white people when they say something that could be construed as racist. They act as if even if I am in the vicinity of sugar I will come out in hives. Diabetes is not a fear of pudding, or an allergy to chocolate. Imagine how pathetic I would feel if that were the case. I would live a life of fear, terrified of a lurking assassin armed with nothing but a Mini Milk.

Here's the headline: I can eat whatever I want, whenever I want. The invention of insulin means that I always have a way of dealing with anything that might be thrown up. However, on some occasions, I can't be bothered with the hassle. The hassle of the calculations, the hassle of the potential impact on the rest of my day. Mark my words, though. If you act like I can't have the dessert that you are presenting to everyone else, I will eat twice as much as everyone else. Then I will make my way around the table eating everyone else's one by one until I have had all of the desserts. Then I will go to your fridge and I will eat everything in it, before I slowly walk to your cupboards and down a bag of sugar, manically laughing as I desperately chew my way through it. Yes, doing this will guarantee me a hellish night of diabetic admin, but it will be worth it to prove my point.

There are a few things that do make me think twice before I indulge. I can't stress enough, I *can* eat these things, but sometimes I go into prediction mode and decide that I can't deal with the swooping glucose levels they will leave me with. Fair warning, these are all delicious things. Such is life, there is nothing clean or healthy that causes me issues. Salads and superfoods are just as boring for the diabetic as everyone else. It is only dishes that would be classed as some of the world's most favourite foods that could be considered enemies of diabetic control.

'Enemies' is a bit strong actually. 'Femmes fatales' might be a better term. I want them, I lust after them, even though in the long run they will ruin me. I am a private dick in a film noir, working in my shadowy office. Then, at the door window, I see a silhouette. I know immediately that the silhouette belongs to my ultimate weakness. She will be my undoing, but I can't resist. I know her true intentions, but my carnal lust will win. It always does.

THE TOP THREE FEMMES FATALES OF DIABETIC CONTROL

Carbohydrates

This one hurts. We are consistently told that we need carbs for energy, but whenever I eat them they send my glucose levels haywire and I'm chasing my tail all day. But how can I resist? The worst offenders (of course) are bread, potatoes and rice. You know, the staples of most delicious cuisines worldwide. In fact, these three things would be part of every meal at all times for ever if I was given the choice. But I have to be measured about it.

In order to help, I actually did a carbohydrate-counting course. I was taught how to be able to eat these things and balance my blood glucose levels by calculating the grammage of carbohydrates and how much insulin my body needs to cover the spike. As I've said, this isn't an exact science, but it still put me in a better position for management. The downside is, I now can't help but estimate the carbohydrate content of every food I see. It's like another illness. Where you might see a plate of chips, I see numbers. I am living in a carbohydrate Matrix and I can't escape.

I suppose you could think of it as a skill of sorts, perhaps a party trick. I can look at other people's meals and tell them approximately how many grams of carbs are in it. From experience, though, it's a party trick that doesn't actually go down that well at parties. It tends to 'kill the vibe'. I have a friend who prides himself on being able to guess people's weight just by looking at them. He's impressively accurate, but even less welcome at social events than I am. If only I could convert my carb-counting acumen into card-counting. I'd be loaded, instead of craving bread every day.

I do eat these things, but they are less a part of my life these days. I try to eat lower carbs day to day in an effort to manage my levels. Sometimes, though, you have to have the carbs. Have you tried curry without rice or naan?! It's just creepy. You really feel like you're down on your luck. The other night I tried a burger with no bun. In place of the bread were two pieces of iceberg lettuce. It was, and I mean this, the single wettest food I have ever eaten, including most soups. Never again.

Cocktails

Cocktail menus are a minefield for diabetics. I love the idea of cocktails, but in reality they present multiple problems for me. I swore off drinking my sugar a long time ago – it's simply a waste of my time and effort. It wasn't too hard to relinquish: full-fat fizzy drinks and orange juice were never my greatest loves and their replacements are more than capable of doing the job. When it comes to boozy cocktails, though, it's trickier.

For a start, it's even harder to make the decision in the first place. Most cocktail menus seem to be in an arms race to use ingredients that nobody has ever heard of. It's tricky enough to estimate the carbohydrates in most familiar things, but when I'm confronted with a Negroni made with plum pálinka, sorrel bitters and yuzu mouse droppings, I'm completely at a loss. So, more often than not in a cocktail situation, I have to go to something I understand.

This feels pathetic, of course. Have you any idea how left out you feel while everyone around you is drinking exciting, tropical-looking vases filled with sparklers and whizz-bangers, while you quietly sit among them with a glass of Malbec? You look like you've come straight from a funeral. Sometimes, the temptation gets too much. I feel like I'm in a good enough position blood glucose-wise and order a complicated-sounding drink. In that case, I have to accept my fate with curiosity. I have to look at my rapidly increasing levels and treat it like an experiment. 'Oh, fascinating, turns out that kumquat moonshine is quite sweet! I'll know that for next time, I guess.'

Pizza

Yes, sadly, this is true. I've already documented my love affair with pizza. For a long time I would've classed pizza as my favourite food. I would eat it most days. When I decided to get on top of my diabetic control, however, I made a horrible discovery. Pizza is pretty much the worst possible food for my glucose levels.

This is because it is an unholy combination of carbs and fat. Not to get too technical, but injecting insulin for carbs is fairly straightforward. You make a calculation, inject, and wait. When you add a whole heap of fat to the equation, though, things get complicated. Fat slows down the absorption of carbs. So, if you inject for the carbs in pizza (approximately one whole loaf of bread), you're in trouble and the insulin will crash your levels, only for the carbs to absorb hours later, leaving you high as hell (and not in a good way). So you end up having to inject some insulin before you eat, then more a few hours later, and even then the high levels may persist for much longer. All in all, pizza is a headfuck.

But sometimes you have to make sacrifices for those you love. I still eat pizza, but not every day. Which is probably good advice for everyone, actually. I no longer eat large deep-dish American pizzas, only thin-crust Italian ones. I probably prefer these anyway now, as I am a grown-up, but I do miss the big boys. My regular order used to be a large deep-dish Pepperoni Feast with extra anchovies from Pizza Hut. I preach compromise with diabetes, but this is something I had to ban from my life. There is simply no situation where that would end well. It's the equivalent of me eating a whole Victoria sponge topped with the monthly output of a dairy farm.

I'm going to stop writing about pizzas now, because I might cry.

People often ask me how I eat so much delicious food as a diabetic in a tone that suggests I am a 'bad' diabetic. For a while, I agreed with them. Surely, if I wasn't eating a restrictive and boring diet I must be bad at managing my condition? I freed myself from this notion a long time ago though. I prefer to see all the positives in what I have to deal with every day.

Before I was diagnosed (and for a while after), I did not think about what I was eating. Now, I am forced to look at what I'm putting into my body and the effect that it has. I eat more consciously, however much that makes me sound like a tosspot. I really have to think about what I eat, and whether it's worth it. As such, if I'm going to eat something that takes some work, I will make sure I have the best version of that thing I can find. I no longer just throw down an average burger, or the nearest takeaway. I will seek out the best possible. If I'm going to have to make calculations and risk feeling a bit wonky, I am going to make sure I enjoy the experience that leads me to that as much as possible. So on one level, diabetes makes me a discerning food superhero. On another, more realistic level, diabetes has simply served to make me even more of a food snob than I was when I was seven.

·14

DIGESTIF

The end of a book, like the end of a meal, should leave you feeling satisfied and pleasant. That sense that you got everything you wanted from the experience and that you would recommend it to your friends.

This is not how I feel after most of my meals, certainly not in restaurants. As must have become clear by now, I gorge and over-order. I see almost all opportunities to eat food as my last, and chow down as if a meteor is headed directly for Earth. I don't think this will ever change. I will never be the sort of person who eats until they are pleasantly full or eats to fuel themselves for future activities. Food *is* my daily activity. Food is enough. Some people might think, 'I have three meetings later; I'd better have a light lunch, so I have enough energy.' I am the other way around. If I have a big meal planned, I would rather cut down on the meetings so I can give the food my undivided attention. I will never be a functional eater. The joy I get from food is far too overwhelming. If you took away my ability to eat well and plentifully, I don't really see what the point of life would be. It would be a desolate wasteland stretching out in front of me, with no chance of the comforting respite that good food gives you. I don't know what I would do without the promise of the next exciting and delicious meal being just a few hours away.

I love spending time with loved ones, of course, but these experiences are infinitely enhanced by the presence of good things to eat and drink. What's a birthday without cake, a family get-together without a meal, an afternoon meet-up without coffee and snacks? They're nothing. Food has been present at all the most wonderful moments of my life. I hate to say that these moments would've been different without the food, but I suspect they would've been. That sandwich we ate before I proposed, the pizza at my eighteenth birthday, the spicy chicken I ate before every tour date in 2022. Just thinking of these foods transports me back to those wonderful times. Food has the ability to make you feel like a child again, to remind you of your family, to whisk you away on holidays you took years ago. This is why I will never abandon my passion for food. We are increasingly told what we should eat, to eat 'healthier', to start following a 'food pyramid'. I say reject that. Live your life. We only have one, and I'd like to spend mine with a full belly, sauce around my mouth and a massive grin across my face.

So, maybe this is the first book where the author hopes you haven't ended it feeling satisfied and pleasant. I hope you've binged this book. I hope you've feasted on every chapter, reading far too much than was advisable, and taken in every word greedily, without taking a second to chew it over. If you are polishing off this book with a little bit of shame, feeling slightly nauseous and as if you can't imagine ever reading a book again, then I have done my job.

ACKNOWLEDGEMENTS

Thank you first and foremost to the Nando's cockerel, Colonel Sanders, The Hamburglar, the Honey Monster and Coco the Monkey. Your hard work and dedication to the dinner tables of the nation will never be forgotten. RIP, of course, to Rik Ricicle, whom we lost to a tragic airlock malfunction on a space mission in 1989. Forever in our hearts.

No less important, I suppose, are my family and friends – who have been invaluable in the creation of this book. Thank you for letting me mine my experiences with you for profit and sorry for not asking. To my mum, Anne: I'm not sure you'll ever read this, because it's not in the No. 1 Ladies' Detective Agency series. But your love and support mean everything to me and nothing I've ever done would be possible without them and you. To my dad, Andrew: you are a constant inspiration to me and I look forward to becoming more and more like you every day. Extra thanks to my dad and my stepmum, Julie, for bringing Kathryn and Patrick into the world – I'm so proud of them as both siblings and dear friends.

To my friends in comedy and out – Nish, James, Amy, Jenny, Tanz, Brett, Nick, Chloe, Tom, Pete, Lou, all of the LBs, everyone at GBM, The Great Benito and everyone at Plosive, James Taylor and everyone at Avalon, tour manager Paul Brown / Linda, and of course Henry Vines and everyone at Transworld who has made this book possible.

Finally, my wife, Charlie, who has had to listen to me empty my head about this book over and over again. You're the best thing that's ever happened.

Ed Gamble is an award-winning stand-up comedian, writer and podcaster. He is co-host of the mega-hit *Off Menu* podcast, and a judge on *Great British Menu*. He is also the co-presenter of Radio X's Sunday-morning show with Matt Crosby.

Ed has featured in stand-up appearances on *Live at the Apollo*, *The Royal Variety Performance*, *The Russell Howard Hour*, and on the US TV show *Conan*. In August 2019, Ed's first stand-up special, *Blood Sugar*, was released as an Amazon Prime original in 200 countries worldwide. Ed's latest tour show, *Electric*, had a twice-extended sell-out UK run.